SHOPS

JOHN GL

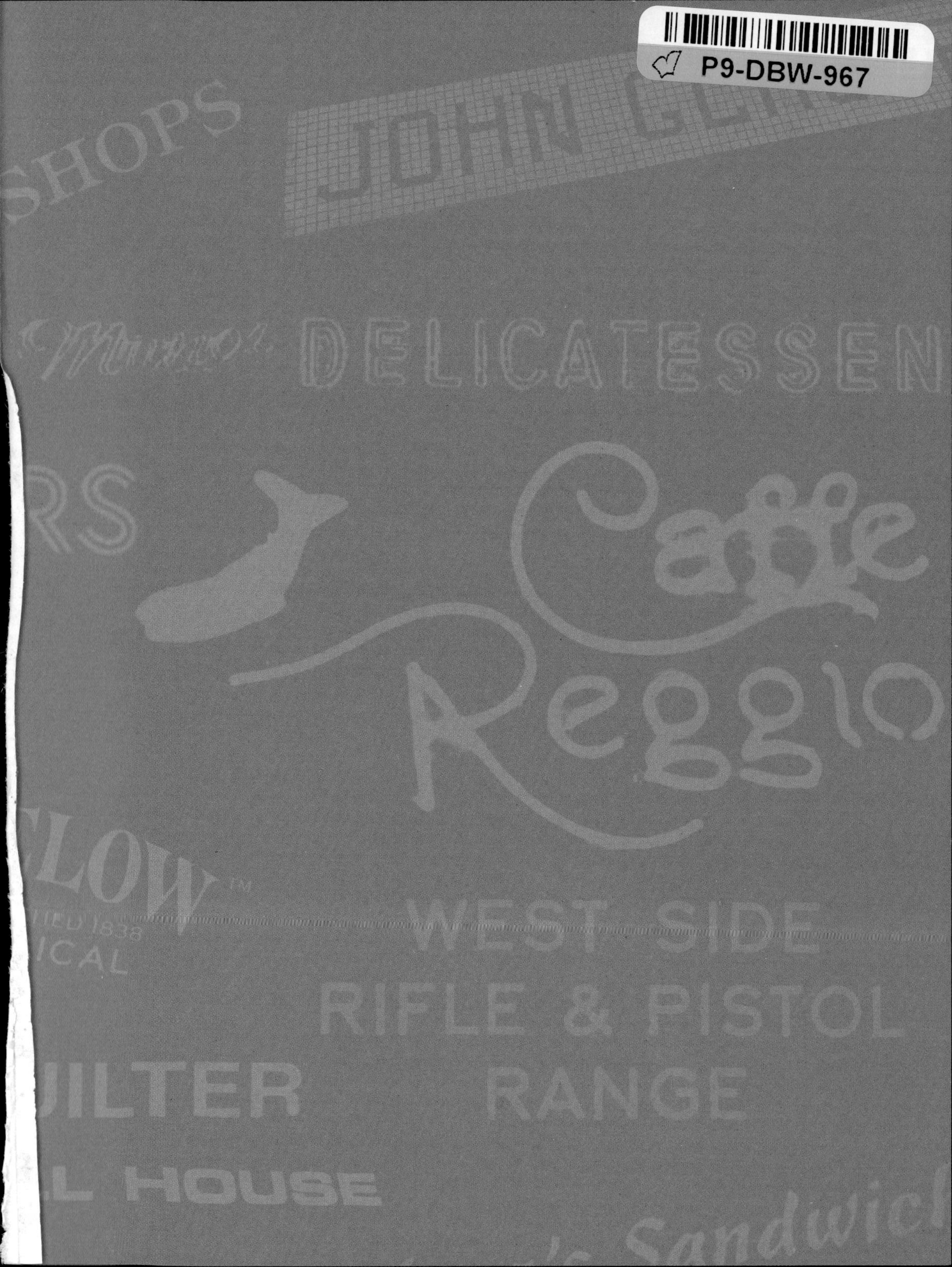

DELICATESSEN

Caffe

Reggio

LOW™

ED 1838

ICAL

WEST SIDE

RIFLE & PISTOL

RANGE

UILTER

L HOUSE

Sandwic

NEW YORK
Originals

NEW

Orig

A GUIDE TO THE
CITY'S CLASSIC

YORK
inals

SHOPS & MOM-AND-POPS

by JAMIE MCDONALD

UNIVERSE

Published by Universe Publishing
A Division of Rizzoli
International Publications, Inc.
300 Park Avenue South
New York, NY 10010
www.rizzoliusa.com

Project Editor: Candice Fehrman
Book Design: Willy Wong
Text and Photography: Jamie McDonald

P. 10, left, second from top: © Leslie Hassler

2012 2013 2014 2015 /
10 9 8 7 6 5 4 3 2 1

Printed in China

ISBN-13: 978-0-7893-2445-0

Library of Congress Catalog Control
Number: 2012932099

Jamie McDonald is the creator and
host of the Emmy Award–winning
television series *New York Originals*,
which has aired on more than 40
PBS stations across the country.
McDonald is a former producer
and has worked at Fox News and
CBS. He began his television career
as a CBS page on *Late Show with
David Letterman*. Jamie grew
up in Indiana, but has lived in
New York City for more than 15
years. He is always on the lookout
for more New York Originals.

Season 1 of the documentary *New
York Originals* is available to order
on a set of three DVDs. This includes
all 10 episodes, which is more
than four hours of footage profiling
45 New York businesses. Visit
www.newyorkoriginalsonline.com
for more information.

THIS BOOK IS DEDICATED TO
MARY GASSER AND CAROL MCDONALD.

TABLE of CONTENTS

MANHATTAN

MANHATTAN CONTINUED

QUEENS

STATEN ISLAND

The idea for *New York Originals* came to me during a visit to my hometown in Indiana. Driving through Noblesville, I saw a street lined with the kinds of chain stores and franchises you see in almost any American city these days—CVS, Starbucks, Best Buy, Wendy's—the list goes on and on. There was nothing special about this particular stretch of road. In fact, if I blindfolded someone and dropped him here, he wouldn't know if he was in Indiana, Oklahoma, or Florida. But I realized all of these chain stores also exist within a five-block radius of my home in New York City—Midtown Manhattan to be exact, the self-proclaimed capital of culture and originality.

All New Yorkers know what I'm talking about. The homogenizing of our city and the loss of many of its original small businesses, some of which have been around for generations, has been happening for a while now. The national chains offer many positives: consistency, service, and—most importantly—low prices. But there are cultural costs as well. For example, a place like Olive Garden isn't going to have lift-up seats that were used to hide alcohol during Prohibition like Old Town Bar; CVS isn't going to have a pharmacist assist you in choosing the exact right medicine like C. O. Bigelow; and T.G.I. Friday's isn't going to attract celebrity customers like Patsy's Pizzeria, Sammy's Roumanian Steakhouse, or really any of the shops and restaurants mentioned in this book.

Decades ago, most small towns sold out their town squares in favor of cheaper and more convenient megastores on the outskirts of the city. People began to forget that the corner coffee shop or local shoe store provided not only goods and services, but also a small part of their community's uniqueness and character. New York City is ironically one of the last vestiges of small-town America. Small businesses like butcher shops, ethnic delis, and corner pubs have a better chance of surviving here than anywhere else in the country. Where else but the Big Apple can someone run into a luncheonette and order an egg cream to go? Or make their own paint from pure pigment? Or buy a baseball glove at the same small sports shop the Yankees use? Some streets in Brooklyn and Queens even have

INTRODUCTION

by Jamie McDonald

the look and feel of the 1950s, with independent small businesses lining the avenues.

There are a few reasons for this. First, New York is a pedestrian society, where one is forced to shop small. Second, immigrants and their descendants keep neighborhood traditions and businesses afloat. But I wanted to know more, so I decided to explore these businesses—and their owners and customers—through *New York Originals*, a half-hour television show that aired on PBS. In doing so, I learned that New Yorkers themselves deserve credit for the large number of these small shops still in existence. New Yorkers know they live in the most unique city in the world and that many of the city's shops and restaurants could only survive here. Customers are loyal; they realize have a direct effect on whether or not a 60-year-old business will be around for another 60 years. They purchase their coffee from a local diner, even though it does not taste exactly the same every day. They order a sandwich from a corner deli, even though it does not look like the perfect ones in Subway advertisements. They take their picture frames and fountain pens to be repaired by specialists, even though it may be cheaper to just buy new ones.

Doing this show also introduced me to the owners of these businesses, who literally live and breathe their work. Many work tirelessly in order to keep their family's legacy alive, even if it doesn't turn a profit. Sometimes loyal employees work at the same shop for decades, and in some cases, even take over the business when the owner is ready to sell or retire. These businesses may look like just another shop or bakery, but for the owners, families, and employees, they stand as an artistic expression to the world.

The *New York Originals* television series aired on more than 40 stations across the country and won an Emmy award in 2011. Now, I am sharing my experiences with these places and their fascinating histories through the pages of this book, which explores and celebrates 75 mom-and-pop businesses in all five boroughs of New York City. It is a book is for all Americans—from New York to Noblesville—who understand and appreciate small businesses and the people who run them.

Candy

LUNCHEONETTE

BAMONTE'S

Pastosa

MPLETE TRAVELLER
BOOK STORE

RESTAURANT

Nom Wah Tea Parlor
谷 餅 裝 華 南 窰 茶 畢 南

DENIGRIS MONUMENTS

Worth & Worth
Worth

FOUNTAIN P

BRONX

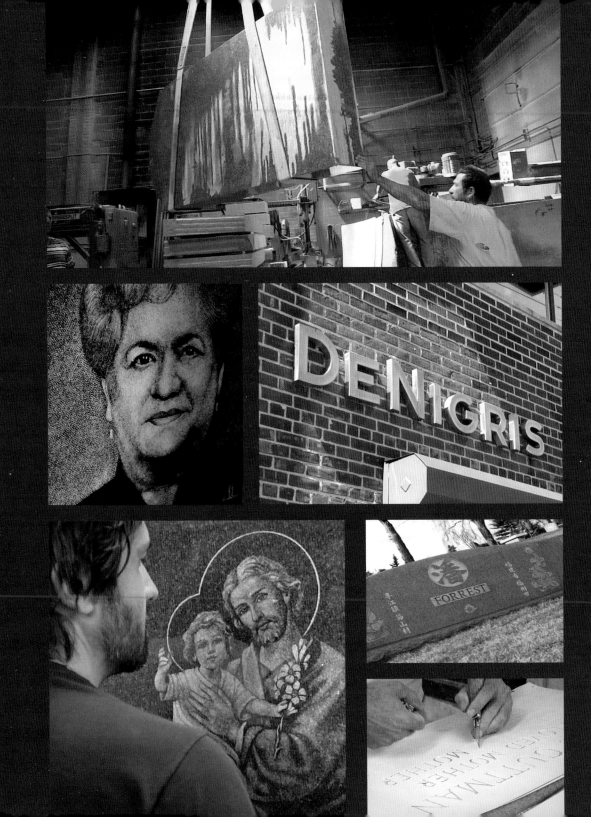

DOMENICK DENIGRIS
MONUMENTS

Established in 1910

1485 Bassett Avenue, Pelham Parkway, Bronx
www.denigrismonuments.com
718-597-4460
Subway: 6 train to Middletown Road
Open by appointment only

It is quite a heady thing to ponder, but for many people the only item they leave on this earth is their headstone. Domenick DeNigris Monuments in the Bronx has been creating these monuments for New Yorkers for several generations.

As wholesale fabricators, DeNigris specializes in monuments and mausoleums, providing them to more than 500 cemeteries in four states. From simple markers for beloved pets to intricately constructed mausoleums, DeNigris designs, executes, and delivers the monuments using a combination of old-world techniques and modern technologies. The company produces some 10,000 monuments a year for all religious denominations and cultural backgrounds.

The process starts with bringing in enormous blocks of granite from Rock of Ages Quarry in Barre, Vermont—well known for its high quality, uniformity, and easy workability. Everything is done in-house in the company's workshop in the Pelham Parkway section of the Bronx. Skylights cast sunlight on a myriad of different sized granite slabs waiting to be carved and shaped. The sounds of stone being hammered and cut continuously echo through the cavernous space. It is not unusual to see 20,000 pounds of granite chunks floating above on a crane just feet over one's head as the rocks travel to workstations for cutting and carving.

The monuments are first designed on a computer, with appropriate lettering and symbols laid out with a pattern. (A prominent sign is posted nearby: "Make sure to check all spellings!") Once a pattern is made, the granite is cut to specifications, and then lettering and symbols are carved, etched, or sandblasted into the stone.

The layman might think working on headstones daily would be a grim occupation. Not so, for the workshop has the air of pleasantness of any well-working workshop. Men busily work on projects, occasionally stopping to tease a fellow co-worker or maybe talk about sports. As company president Donald DeNigris said, "I think what the people who work here are really interested in is making a product that will satisfy the customer. They don't really think about death." His brother and co-owner, Phil DeNigris, said this was not the case right after September 11, though. "We'd start seeing a lot of birth dates from the 1950s and '60s, and that kind of took its toll," he said. "Also, it is never easy when it is a child. There is no way around that, no way around that at all."

DeNigris was founded back in 1910 by Donald and Phil's grandfather, Domenick DeNigris, who started as a granite builder who made items such as stairs, fascias, and building components. When the Depression hit, work dried up, so he changed gears and began mining granite wholesale and making monuments. Today, the DeNigris brothers run the business along with their sons and nephews, making it a four-generation enterprise. In typical brother fashion, the two seem nothing alike. Donald is the salesman, dressed to the nines, and Phil is in charge of the workshop, looking more like an old-world craftsman.

With all these decades under its belt, DeNigris has quite an illustrious history. Its work includes Monument Park at Yankee Stadium, jazz musician Miles Davis's headstone in New York's Woodlawn Cemetery, and, more recently, Les Paul's memorial in Wisconsin.

Watching the shop's industrial stonecutter in action is worth the trip alone. Slabs of granite—thousands of pounds each—are slid into the machine. Metal blades acting much like front teeth come down on the granite, snapping the stone apart with 300 tons of pressure. The resulting "crack" can sound like a small explosion.

Like any other industry, technological advances have allowed for all kinds of innovations in monument fabrication.

Along with the good old hammer and chisel, DeNigris also uses cutting-edge technologies like diamond saws to cut stones as easily as wood, and sandblasting for lettering, which uses a computer-generated synthetic relief overlay that results in astonishingly great detail.

Recent trends in monuments include etching the stone. According to Phil, it caught on due to Eastern European immigrants, since it is very popular in places like Russia. Using just a Dremel tool and steel picks to carve, artisans can create portraits on the stone that have the tone and depth of a photograph. Another trend is personalizing headstones. Images of the deceased's favorite hobbies, cars, celebrities, sports teams, or even rock bands are common. DeNigris has even carved The Three Stooges into a monument.

According to Donald DeNigris, it is always important for a grave to be marked. "Essentially, a marker is for the family of the deceased. People go through a lot when somebody passes, and it's not until that monument or marker is on the gravesite that the final closure comes. The memorial is kind of the last say; it brings closure."

FRANK BEE

Established in 1957

3435 East Tremont Avenue
Throg's Neck, Bronx
www.frankbeecostume.com
718-823-9792
Subway: 6 train to
Westchester Square–East Tremont Avenue
Bus: BX40 or BX42 bus to
East Tremont Avenue–Bruckner Boulevard
Hours vary

The five-and-ten store is just as endangered as the soda fountain and drive-in theater, but up in the Bronx there is one five-and-ten—Frank Bee—that is still alive and kicking, selling hardware, notions, and just about anything else a household could need. "It's not a cookie cutter store," said co-owner Wayne Baker. "We're a dying breed."

Wayne—along with his brother and co-owner Douglas—currently runs Frank Bee. Their father, Arthur Baker, started the store in 1957. "My uncle Frank lent my father $10,000 to open up the business," explained Wayne Baker. "So my father named the store after Uncle Frank."

From the tin ceiling to the wood floors, the place lives and breathes small-town America of days past. A visit to Frank Bee is not just a nostalgia trip, though. As its bright red-and-white striped awning declares, it is the first place to try for anything. Frank Bee specializes in merchandise you cannot find anywhere else. For example, the store carries classic cleaning products, like Carbona Liquid Spot Remover, and specialized kitchen utensils, like banana cutters and stovetop coffeepots. There is also ribbon by the foot, sewing thread and needles, knitting yarn, hardware, underwear, clotheslines and slotted clothespins, a wide variety of gadgets, and even brand-new wooden and tin washboards.

Most chain stores won't sell certain items if they can't guarantee to sell a certain amount. At Frank Bee, the Baker brothers like to be able to offer these hard-to-find objects. "We have a tendency to hold onto things," said Baker. "We probably keep some things a little too long, but eventually everything sells." According to the brothers, when a customer asks about a random item, Frank Bee has a 95 percent success rate of having it in stock. And if it doesn't, well, Frank Bee has another motto: "If We Don't Have It, You Don't Need It."

One of the ways Frank Bee manages to hold on through this era of big-box chain stores is by diversifying. It now has a store specializing in uniforms, a costume business, and a rental service. One of the largest of its kind in New York, the rental service has provided items to carnivals, costumes to *Saturday Night Live* and Oprah Winfrey, and even tents to President Barack Obama's election campaign.

Still, as successful as these enterprises have been, the brothers' true love will always be the five-and-ten. It isn't the biggest revenue generator of the business, but the brothers really keep it going as a tribute to their father. Plus, something the variety store has always had is loyalty, from both its employees and its customers. "The nice part about it," said Baker, "is wherever I am, whether I'm in Florida on vacation, with my family, or in an obscure place, somebody will come up to me and say, 'Aren't you from Frank Bee?'"

FRANK'S SPORTS SHOP

Established in 1922

430 East Tremont Avenue, Tremont, Bronx
www.frankssports.com
718-299-9628
Subway: B or D train to Tremont Avenue
Open Monday–Friday: 9:00 a.m. to 7:45 p.m.
Saturday: 9:00 a.m. to 6:45 p.m.
Closed Sunday

Sporting goods stores are yet another business that has suffered as a result of the big-box chain store phenomenon. Yet, up in the Bronx of all places, one family-owned sports shop is still thriving—Frank's Sports Shop. Its location is proof that it must be doing something right. A bit out of the way on East Tremont Avenue, the store still manages to attract shoppers from all over the world.

Owner Moe Stein, a spry man in his 80s, is part of the appeal. An absolute expert in sporting goods and a bit of a ham, he is practically a fixture here—holding court in the middle of the store, working the phones, helping customers, and ribbing his employees. "If you stay near the door, I will guarantee within five minutes somebody will come in and say, 'My father brought me here,' or 'My grandfather brought me here,' and they'll have their own kid with them. I'll always go shake the hand of the kid and say, 'You're the most important thing. You're tomorrow's money, so I got to be nice to you,'" said Stein, chuckling.

Stein has called this part of the Bronx home pretty much his whole life, even working at the store as a little boy. Stein's father, Frank, opened Frank's Sports Shop in 1919. It was originally located on the Bowery in Manhattan, but moved to its current location in 1922. The move was an unusual one, but it worked. "Someone had told my father that tomorrow's world would be in the Bronx and he should move there and that's where we are today. Ninety years, same location, same people," said Stein.

Frank's prides itself on stocking obscure and hard-to-find items that chain stores often ignore, like fishing and archery supplies, unusual shoe sizes, and camping supplies. Frank's also sells uniforms to the New York Sanitation Department, postal workers, and even the Boy Scouts. Plus, there are a few products here that one would probably never expect to see for sale in the Bronx, much less in the rest of New York City: firearms and ammo. Frank's has always had a full line of hunting equipment. It even issues hunting and fishing licenses and offers safety courses at no charge. "There's no reason not to sell these items," said Stein. "We don't kill people and our customers don't kill people. I mean, if you want to figure out the odds of who's getting shot by who, it doesn't work out that the guy with the license is going to end up shooting somebody."

Like any good business, Frank's knows what keeps people coming back the most—good service and great prices. "We don't mark goods up to mark goods down," said Stein. "We carry goods at very competitive prices and

complete
GUN
TREATMENT

HUNTERS
BODY + HAIR
SOAP

you can walk out knowing that you're doing the right thing." And let's not forget the customer service. The salespeople at Frank's are not just kids at an after-school job, but rather career specialists, some of whom have been working here for decades. This is just one of the reasons even professional athletes shop here, including Yankee players Alex Rodriguez and Derek Jeter and boxer Muhammad Ali, among others.

"Funny story about Ali," continued Stein. "He was buying some stuff, and he came in with a guard. Meanwhile, the guard was buying a shotgun. The guard said to the salesperson, 'If you don't finish the paperwork in time, I'm out the door, because when Ali goes, I go.' We had to hold Ali here, so I got the kids talking to him. That was a tricky one, trying to keep Ali occupied long enough so we could finish the sale with his guard."

Another great story is when Frank's helped Yankee Stadium in a pinch. Another team was in town for a double-header, and one of its players had lost his uniform. When Stein received the call, he rushed the store's seamstress over to sew a name and number to an extra shirt. "The Almighty must have been looking out for that team, because it was one of the longest games in history," said Stein. "If we hadn't helped, that pitcher would have gone on without his name and number."

It is not surprising that Stein has so many great stories, for he works 60 hours a week and has no thought of retiring. "We had a magazine come in to interview us," said Stein. "The interviewer said, 'Can I ask you one question? What do you attribute your success to?' I had to think about it. I finally figured it out—all my competitors died."

Jokes aside, what Stein really enjoys about running the shop are all the people who come through the door. "These are people I've known for 30 or 40 years. I can't describe it, but it means a lot, and they are all friends."

JJ BURCK
MARINE SUPPLIES

Established in 1928

526 City Island Avenue, City Island, Bronx
718-885-1559
Bus: BX29 to City Island Avenue–Cross Street
Open Sunday–Friday: 9:00 a.m. to 6:00 p.m.
Saturday: 8:00 a.m. to 4:30 p.m.

City Island has been called the Cape Cod of New York. With its waterfront views and quaint storefronts, one could easily mistake it for a New England fishing village. Easily accessed by car or city bus, it is worlds apart from the rest of metropolitan New York in both spirit and look. Just one square mile in size, the island is a quiet residential enclave known today for its seafood restaurants and pleasure boating activities.

That's where JJ Burck Marine Supplies comes in. Since the 1920s, this little shop has been helping leisurely boaters make the most of the sea, while also giving them a place to tell a fish tale or two. Now in its third generation of ownership, JJ Burck was opened in 1928 by Joseph Burck. His son and grandson—both named Joe—now run things. The son remembers spending his summers at the shop as a kid in the 1950s. "I could remember getting a quarter for carrying something out to the car for customers and I thought it was a million dollars," he said.

Located on the island's main drag, City Island Avenue, JJ Burck specializes in almost any kind of boating supply imaginable: anchors, lines, paints, waxes, motor parts, oils, greases—anything customers need for their sailboat, powerboat, jet ski, or even kayak. Weekend mornings are the busiest for JJ Burck. The place fills quickly with boaters gathering up supplies, eagerly anticipating their day on the sea. It is one of those places filled with so much bric-a-brac that customers go in looking for one item and come out with a dozen.

Even if boating is not your thing, JJ Burck is worth a visit, for it is one of those quaint old shops where time has seemingly stopped. The building itself was built in 1876, and many of its original fixtures are still intact. There is the original plank wood floor that creaks with every step, as well as the ornate tin ceiling and vintage wainscoting painted in a unique glossy yellow and blue motif. Lining the walls are photographs of the City Island of days past, not to mention photos of a few proud men with their daily catches.

What is the secret to the business's longevity? "Just hard work," said Burck. "And you have to like what you're doing." One thing Burck has learned over the years is that the good old days were not necessarily better. Since boats and motors are more reliable today, boaters can go on longer trips without any worries. That said, not much else has changed over the years. "It's basically the same," said Burck. "Fishermen just lie bigger about the fish."

WELCOME TO
CITY ISLAND
SETTLED 1685

The
GARDEN CLUB
of
CITY ISLAND

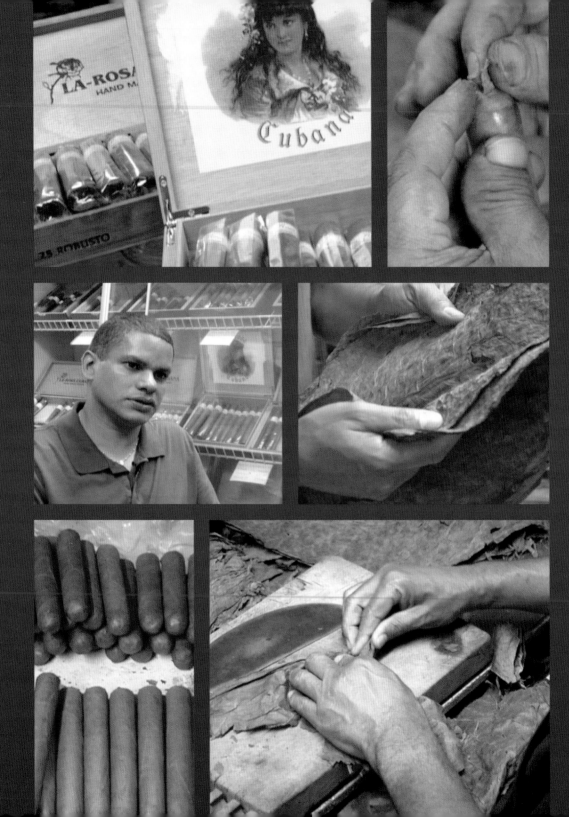

When you enter La Rosa Cubana Cigars, you will be transported to another era—a place where craftsmen still practice the old-world trade of hand rolling cigars. Inside the smoky, auburn-tinged space, one can smell the rich scent of tobacco as rollers craft their cigars on small work tables right before customers' eyes.

Cigar rolling factories were at one time a booming industry in New York City. According to owner Frank Almanzar, there used to be more than 20 in the city, but now only four remain. La Rosa Cubana Cigars used to be located in Midtown Manhattan, but it recently moved to the Bronx. It was founded in 1958 by Almanzar's father, A. Antonio Almanzar, who named his brand after his daughter. Frank Almanzar took over the business after his father passed away, but not before a long tutelage; he first apprenticed at the shop when he was just 12 years old. Now, Almanzar's son George pitches in, along with many longtime workers and family members.

La Rosa Cubana Cigars offers several different kinds of cigars and will take special orders custom-made to a customer's specifications—varying the type of tobacco, thickness, length, or even shape as desired. Because the cigars are made in-house, they are moderately priced; just a few dollars buys a top-notch smoke.

La Rosa's master rollers learn their craft in the Dominican Republic, which has just as much tradition and excellence in cigar manufacturing as Cuba. A good cigar roller can make more than 200 cigars a day, about one every two to three minutes. "The difference is that you got the guys rolling right on the spot," said Almanzar. Not only do people enjoy seeing how the cigars are rolled, they also get a fresher, moister cigar that has a rich and peppery taste.

Also helping to create that unique flavor are La Rosa's multinational ingredients. Because of the U.S. embargo against Cuba, the shop uses Cuban tobacco seeds that are grown in the Dominican Republic, giving the tobacco the best of both worlds. Plus, the outer leaves used to wrap the tobacco are actually grown in Connecticut. This may come as a surprise, but many high-end cigar manufacturers use tobacco grown in the Connecticut River Valley and parts of Massachusetts due to this region's unique soil.

La Rosa cigars are first made by bunching up a combination of different flavored leaves, which are then wrapped in an inner tobacco leaf. This mixture is put into a cigar mold, which is later put into a hydraulic press for about an hour. The hundreds of pounds of pressure is what gives the cigars their initial shape. Next, an outer leaf is carefully wrapped around the cigar, cut to shape, and tapered on the ends. Only then is a cigar ready for the La Rosa cigar band, a band that Almanzar makes sure represents quality and family.

"It's the taste," said one longtime customer, when asked what he liked about La Rosa cigars. "Each cigar is different because the hand makes it different. They're uniform, but not exactly uniform. That's what makes it art, like a painting."

THE CITY O

TINY D

BROOKLYN
STABLES

ONIEA
GRAND STE

Lexington
Candy Shop
LUNCHEONETTE

BAMONTE'S

Pastosa

MPLETE TRAVELLER
BOOK STORE

RESTAURANT

Mellah Tea Parlor

BROOKLYN

BAMONTE'S

Established in 1900

32 Withers Street, Williamsburg, Brooklyn
718-384-8831
Subway: G train to Metropolitan Avenue
or L train to Lorimer Street
Open Monday, Wednesday, and Thursday:
12:00 p.m. to 10:00 p.m.
Friday and Saturday:
12:00 p.m. to 11:00 p.m.
Closed Tuesday

Dare it be said that Bamonte's is the holy grail of Italian restaurants in America. Long before this country embraced Italian cuisine, even pizza for that matter, there was Bamonte's. Not only was it one of the first Italian restaurants in the United States, it is also one of New York City's oldest restaurants. Opened in 1900, the same family has cared for it all this time. In its fourth generation of ownership, three sisters—Laura, Lisa, and Nicole Bamonte—have taken the reins while their relatives watch on proudly.

Bamonte's longevity is partly due to its fiercely loyal clientele. And with the hipsterfication of Williamsburg, Bamonte's is also being discovered by its new and younger neighbors, who view it as a respite from the area's trendy bars and restaurants or just a reminder of Sunday night family dinners. On any given night, the dining room hosts twentysomethings as well as families from the old neighborhood.

Considering the restaurant's location, this loyalty is even more amazing. Sandwiched between two townhouses, it is the only commercial business on the block; its lighted sign is a unique beacon on an otherwise quiet residential street.

Withers Street is a forgotten stretch of North Williamsburg, an Italian American enclave gutted decades ago by the Brooklyn-Queens Expressway that now runs through it. With little evidence of its former self, save a couple of ethnic churches and organizations, Bamonte's serves as one of the last pieces of this former immigrant neighborhood. Nightly, patrons come from down the street, other parts of Brooklyn, or even Manhattan, Long Island, and New Jersey not just for a taste of the old country but also the old neighborhood. One longtime customer said, "I have been coming here now for 50 years. My parents took me here. When you walk in here, you smell the garlic odor in the walls. That's how great it is. We have been to Manhattan, gone to high-end restaurants, but this is just being home."

In fact, many customers comment on how Bamonte's, which has changed very little over the years, feels like walking back into their youth. Looking much like Grandma's living room, Bamonte's interior is wonderfully mid-century American. There is dark wood paneling throughout the place, brass chandeliers, and deep red carpeting and drapes. Photographs of several generations of the Bamonte

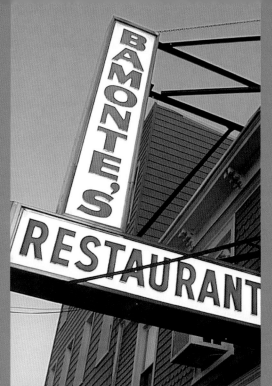

family fill the walls. "We got a review once and they said it's like walking into a time capsule. If we changed the decor, I don't think people would feel the same," said Lisa Bamonte.

It is Bamonte's kitchen, however, that takes center stage—figuratively and literally. It is one of the first open-windowed kitchens, conceived way before trendy contemporary restaurants thought the idea was chic. The family had always kept a clean kitchen and wanted to show it off, so in 1950 they converted it to the open-window format. "We've had people so into it that they just walk right into the kitchen and watch their meal being prepared. They think it's amazing," said Bamonte.

As an unapologetic classic red sauce restaurant, Bamonte's has collected rave reviews, including one from the Zagat Survey—not easy in a town always looking for the next best thing. Specializing in Neapolitan cuisine, entrees include mussels marinara, linguine with crab sauce, zuppa di clams, and veal pizzaiola. And for dessert there is cheesecake, apple crumb pie, and berry cream pie, all baked by Laura Bamonte.

Service is big here and it starts right at the door. When you walk in, you'll receive a greeting from the bartender (if you're a regular, he'll already be mixing your drink) or one of the three Bamonte sisters. "It's about the whole atmosphere. When you come into Bamonte's, you are coming into our living room. We want to know if you are having a great dining experience," said Bamonte. Tuxedoed waiters complete the experience, some of which have been here as long as the family members. Many are 20-year veterans, and at least one has 40 years under his belt.

Bamonte's was first opened by the sisters' great-grandfather, Pasquale Bamonte, a newly emigrated piano maker from Italy. He opened the place first as a catering hall and called it Liberty Hall, probably out of appreciation for his new country. For years, it was a meeting place used for banquets, weddings, and the occasional political event. Then in 1950, he changed the name to Bamonte's and dedicated the restaurant to Italian cuisine. There was even a bocce ball court in the back where customers could play while waiting for their food.

For years, Bamonte's was an after-game clubhouse for the Brooklyn Dodgers. Lou Durocher, Pee Wee Reese, and many other players were regulars; they mingled side-by-side with regular folks, fans, and the famed Brooklyn Dodger Sym-Phony Band. Bamonte's other brushes with fame include being used as a backdrop for several movies and television shows, including *Kojak* and a few episodes of *The Sopranos*. Harrison Ford, Jack Nicholson, Tommy Lasorda, and Anjelica Houston have all dined here. Even Yankee great Joe DiMaggio used to be a regular. "He would fly in from the airport and come and have dinner. He was very approachable. He was a very special man to us," said Laura Bamonte.

Just as Bamonte's is a special place to so many people. And now that the sisters have taken over, their father can enjoy the fruits of his labor. How is it having three sisters working together? "The three of us have three different personalities, but we mesh very well together," said Lisa Bamonte.

But the biggest reward, according to Lisa, is making their father proud. "To have your dad turn around and say that he is proud of you is one of the biggest accomplishments. He has given up so much of his life to make a better life for us, so for us to continue the tradition is a great gift to give back to him."

Soggy and drippy may not sound like good words to describe a top-notch meal, but when you are talking about roast beef sandwiches, it is a ringing endorsement. Brennan and Carr in Sheepshead Bay, Brooklyn, has been serving these beefy beauties since the 1930s, and they are some of the most tender and flavorful roast beef sandwiches in the city.

Walking down Nostrand Avenue, one can't help but notice the restaurant. Its Old English Tudor-style facade sticks out of an otherwise bland strip of chain stores. It is fitting in a way, for this is a special place, a place that makes a cuisine that is often tried but rarely done properly. Sure, one can get a roast beef sandwich just about anywhere, but not one like this—made the right way with the right cut and quality of beef and prepared in the time-intensive way that makes it so tender and flavorful.

The rest of Brennan and Carr's menu is a comfort food hall of fame, including pie à la mode, clam chowder, and grilled hamburgers, which are freshly ground in-house and never frozen, giving them a taste bud–popping flavor.

Brennan and Carr's dining area is perfectly suited for its food. It is a cozy wood dining room reminiscent of a den in a 1950s home. "We've kept the nostalgia of the restaurant," said general manager Eddie Sullivan. "The type of place that we are, you know, we're not neon signs and fancy lights, we are who we are." Customers like that the place hasn't changed much.

George Brennan and Edward Carr—two carpenters by trade looking for a more reliable income—opened Brennan and Carr in 1938. At the time, Sheepshead Bay was still a rural spot, so they ran the restaurant as a takeout place. Over the decades, the business grew and the two carpenters built a dining room, quickly establishing a reputation as a roast beef legend. In 1970, Eddie Sullivan's father, John Sullivan, bought the place. He had spent years working here as a kid and loved the place.

Luckily for us, the Sullivans have been meticulous about keeping the roast beef sandwiches exactly the same. It starts with a top shelf cut of beef. Like many of the great restaurants in New York City, Brennan and Carr is very particular about the meat it purchases. "We've been buying the same meat for many years, from the same family, so there's a lot of trust built up there on the product that we're bringing in," said Sullivan.

Three times a week, the shop gets deliveries of boneless top rounds. Each side of beef is then carefully trimmed to give it just enough fat content. Some of the fat is then sliced thin and tied back onto the trimmed beef to help ensure a safe and even cook of the meat. Next, the beef is oven-roasted for one-and-a-half hours at 350 degrees. It is then thinly sliced, ready for its dip in the legendary Brennan and Carr juice tray.

This one-by-four-foot stainless steel flame-heated wonder is filled with juices harnessed from the day's roast beef cooking. A couple of secret ingredients are added, and then the sandwiches are dipped into the trough to saturate the beef in its own flavorful juices. Customers can order a light or soggy dip. Some will go all the way—requesting that the whole sandwich be completely submerged in the juice tray—and then eat it with a knife and fork.

Considering the delicious food, it's not surprising that many people come back here year after year. Some even come in five or six days a week. Over the years, families that have moved over to New Jersey or Long Island will come back to visit, knowing at least one thing is still the same from their old Brooklyn neighborhood: Brennan and Carr.

BRENNAN AND CARR

Established in 1938

3432 Nostrand Avenue
Sheepshead Bay, Brooklyn
www.facebook.com/pages/
Brennan-Carr/412166715533
718-646-9559
Subway: B or Q train to Neck Road
Open Sunday–Thursday:
11:00 a.m. to 1:00 a.m.
Friday–Saturday:
11:00 a.m. to 2:00 a.m.

ROAST
HAMBURGER PLATE
FRENCH FRIES
FRENCH FRIES / CHEESE
FRANK
ONION RINGS
MOZZARRELLA STICKS 525
WING DINGS

BROOKLYN COPPER COOKWARE

Established in 2010

68 Jay Street, Suite 201
Dumbo, Brooklyn
www.brooklyncoppercookware.com
412-267-7371
Subway: F train to York Street
Open by appointment only

To the uninitiated, copper cookware seems like, well, just any cookware. But for cooking aficionados there are two camps: those who use copper cookware and those who don't. "For those who have made the switch it can be rather life-changing," said Mac Kohler, owner of Brooklyn Copper Cookware.

Copper cookware can last for years; it is often passed down from generation to generation. In fact, the Queen of England's kitchen staff still uses cooper cookware that is more than 200 years old. Longevity aside, the cooking properties of copper cookware are second-to-none. Copper gives the user an almost instant and consistent heat, thus the chef has much more control, which is particularly helpful when making delicate sauces and sautés. Plus, copper cookware is just plain beautiful—whether it's gleaming on the stove or simply hanging from the wall.

With all of these selling points, it is a bit surprising that only one company is still making copper cookware in America. Brooklyn Copper Cookware is the brainchild of Mac Kohler. The company—with its workshop in Bushwick and its offices in Dumbo—sells pots and pans ranging from a one-quart saucepan to a 13-quart stockpot and everything in between. Whether you're looking for bakeware, sauté pans,

or casserole dishes, all are handmade, one-of-a-kind pieces.

Brooklyn Copper Cookware is actually the legacy of another business. Back in the 1980s, Jeff Herkes bought an old machine shop in Brooklyn. Inside were the tooling mold parts from the old Bruno Waldrow Copperworks. Beginning in 1936, Bruno Waldrow was the preeminent copper cookware company in America; it rivaled the best of the Belgian and French companies. But thanks in part to the public's sudden infatuation with nonstick Teflon cookware, the company eventually ran out of steam in the 1980s. After some initial testing, Herkes realized that much of the tooling was in tip-top shape, ready to churn out new cookware. With Kohler soon on board, they worked together to reinvigorate the product line.

Today, a small group of craftsmen work out of a 19th-century machine shop in Bushwick. The building is rustic and old-world. Antique machines hum and whirl just as well as their modern counterparts, spinning raw copper into pots of art. The pieces are made one at a time and, depending on size, can take from just a few minutes to almost an hour to shape.

The process starts with a large circle punched out of raw copper sheets. The "penny," as it is called, is mounted on a lathe along with the desired cookware's mold, or "chuck." The lathe spins at a high speed as the machinist uses a greased steel wand to push the copper over the chuck. The process is akin to a parent with a fussy child—the machinist carefully but firmly coaxes the copper into a shape it does not naturally want to hold. While doing so, the machinist is also listening to the copper. As the copper moves up the mold, the friction heats, stretches, and hardens it, causing varying tones as it moves. If the sound gets too high, that means the pot's wall has become too hard or too thin and could break.

After the pot is shaped, a craftsman trims the completed form to its appropriate wall height with a hardened brass blade. Next, it is fitted with a handle. Since each pot is handmade, and thus unique, the handles also have to be made individually for each piece. The tinning, a visually fascinating process, comes next. All cooper cookware has a tin lining to ensure proper heating, to protect ingredients from the copper, and to make washing easier. This process begins with cleaning the pot with acid and then masking the outside with flux to prevent unwanted tin adhesion. The pot is then heated to around 800 degrees. Raw tin is rubbed into the center of the pot much like a stick of butter, crackling as it enters. A wad of cotton batting is then quickly rubbed on the tin, causing the tin to instantly adhere to the copper, resulting in an ultra-smooth and even finish. A quick dip in some cool water causes the metals to form a tight molecular bond. Last, the pot is given a five-step polish. Prices for finished cookware range from around $160 for a one-quart saucepan to $700 for a 13-quart stockpot. The company also re-tins old pots from any manufacturer.

The process to make these copper beauties takes quite a bit of work and money, but the effects are well worth it. "There is a kind of ineffable quality to a handworked piece of anything that is hard to describe in detail, but that's precisely what makes it ineffable," said Kohler.

BUZZ-A-RAMA

Established in 1965

69 Church Avenue, Kensington, Brooklyn
www.buzz-a-rama.com
718-853-1800
Subway: F or G train to Church Avenue
Hours vary

In the 1960s, one of the hottest crazes was slot car racing, which consisted of tabletop racing tracks with little cars that were operated by hand controllers. Like drive-in movie theaters and Tang, this might seem like a dusty old relic of the past, especially in these days of virtual reality racing games and IMAX theaters. But in the sleepy immigrant neighborhood of Kensington, Brooklyn, is a place called Buzz-A-Rama, where not much has changed since Richard Nixon was in office.

During the halcyon days of slot car racing, Buzz-A-Rama was known worldwide as one of the preeminent stops on the slot car racing circuit. Lines outside the door and 24-hour rallies were common, thanks to the hospitality and good-natured fun of Buzz Perri and his wife, Dolores. At one point, there were more than 40 slot car shops in the New York metropolitan area. Now, only Buzz-A-Rama remains.

Buzz-A-Rama has survived all these years thanks to its namesake, Buzz Perri, an energetic man in his seventies who has a quick sense of humor and a patient way with children, who are often overstimulated by the sights and sounds of the racing world. Master of the tracks since 1965, Perri opened his place when the hobby was just taking off. These days, his accountant complains that the building is worth more than the business, but Perri still runs it as a labor of love. On any given weekend, Buzz-A-Rama is packed with all kinds of people: middle-aged men reliving their youth, twentysomethings enjoying the kitschiness of it all, girlfriends humoring their boyfriends, and kids having the time of their lives.

Buzz-A-Rama's expertly designed eight-lane tracks are made for competitive play involving several racers at a time. One track alone could fill up a two-car garage. For a few dollars, even the most inexperienced racer can rent a car and hit the tracks. This is not mere child's play, however; skill is necessary. The key is to go as fast as you can without spinning out. While watching more experienced racers, one can see the almost surgical touch required on the controller when managing sharp banks and turns.

In fact, watching seasoned racers is worth a visit alone. These are not the eccentric characters you may find at a comic book store or sci-fi convention; rather—dare we say—skilled sportsmen who are more than happy to share their world with the uninitiated. These tabletop speed demons are so serious about their hobby that they bring along their own tools and equipment, not to mention custom-made cars and even souped up and tricked out controllers, anything to squeeze every last bit of speed out of the tracks. It is not unheard of for a racer to pump $500 worth of improvements into a car that fits comfortably in the palm of their hand. Just a few small changes like adding new tires, swapping chassis, or perfecting the aerodynamics can make vast differences in a car's performance. And it is all worth it, for watching these cars—little engineering wonders whizzing by at up to 100 miles per hour—is a sight to see.

Buzz and Dolores Perri said they have greatly enjoyed going out in public over the years. Inevitably, a child will recognize them and react as if they have just seen A.J. Foyt or Dale Earnhardt. To this day, when they travel even to the most distant parts of the country, a grown-up will recognize them and fondly recall visiting Buzz-A-Rama as a child. More than a few are heartened, if not amazed, that Buzz-A-Rama is still around. When these former customers return, they marvel at how the place looks exactly the same; they even comment that the smell of the tracks is just how they remember it.

Even more rewarding, however, are the occasions when the Perris have disabled children race at Buzz-A-Rama. Children who cannot walk but are able to manipulate the controllers with their hands suddenly find themselves gaming competitively with their peers. The looks on their faces when they win can bring tears to one's eyes.

It has sometimes been a struggle for Buzz-A-Rama to survive. Having to compete with video games, television, and even home versions of tabletop slot cars, it is amazing the business is still around at all. In the 1970s, the Perris tried a gimmick called the Buzz-A-Rama Bunnies. "Buzz would hire attractive young ladies dressed in Playboy bunny outfits to assist with putting the cars back into the slots after drivers spun out of control," explained Dolores Perri. "The instances of spinouts greatly increased when the bunnies were employed—particularly on father-and-son nights."

Today, the Perris have tapped into the world of event hosting. Parents can rent out the tracks for birthday parties, scouting trips, or other events. (Adult parties are also welcome, but alcohol and profanity are strict no-nos.) There is even a small party room filled with vintage arcade games from the Perris' personal collection. Slot car racing is a wonderful family outing, for it is one of those activities at which children can actually beat their parents. The Perris love watching the joyful faces of satisfied children who come out ahead of their parents during a hard-fought race. And that is proof enough that some places in New York City should survive just for the fun of it.

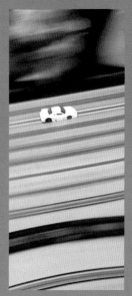

EMBEE SUNSHADE COMPANY

Established in 1933

722 Metropolitan Avenue No. 1, Williamsburg, Brooklyn
www.embeesunshade.com 718-387-8566
Subway: L train to Graham Avenue
Open Monday–Friday: 9:00 a.m. to 5:00 p.m.

These days, most people think of Williamsburg, Brooklyn, as hipster central—a place to be seen or maybe pick up an organic something or other. There was a time, however, when its industrial buildings were not filled with loft apartments and boutiques. It was an era when Brooklyn was one of the manufacturing capitals of the world. Some of those manufacturers still exist, and they are still making goods you probably see every day. The Embee Sunshade Company, creators of classic large umbrellas, is one such business. Not only is it one of the oldest umbrella manufacturers in the world, it is also the last still making its product in America.

Embee Sunshades are a classic fixture in New York City: on beaches, at cafés, and in parks, not to mention on every street cart in the Big Apple. They range from five-and-a-half feet to a gargantuan 10 feet in diameter, and are made of rugged canvas and aluminum. Known for their high quality and durability, the umbrellas are custom-made for each customer. "If somebody wants something with a specific color combination, we can do it for them," said co-owner Barnett Brickner, who runs the company with his cousin, Herbert. "A lot of times decorators want umbrellas for customers with a specific pattern and they will send us material. As a matter of fact, about three years ago someone called us from Oprah Winfrey's magazine. She wanted an umbrella with a certain design on it and we made it for her." And Oprah's people are not the only ones who have come calling. Embee umbrellas are all over the place—from New York City's parks system to a scene in a Woody Allen movie.

Brickner's grandfather, Morris Brickner, came here as a Polish immigrant in the early 1900s and started a rain umbrella business on the Lower East Side. His two sons, George and Max, learned the trade, and then in 1933 they formed the Embee Sunshade Company. Since the 1940s, it has managed to stay in the same location—a converted turn-of-the-century horse stable. As Brickner knows, this business is about more than just putting more sunshades on the New York landscape. "A place like this is the backbone of the whole economy," he said. "We serve a purpose. We're part of the cog in the economy of the city." And as more manufacturing jobs move overseas, Embee has managed to keep production of its sunshades in the United States by keeping a group of uniquely skilled craftsmen on staff.

"It's hard to compete [with overseas manufacturers] because if you want quality, you have to pay for quality," said Brickner. "All of our materials cost more. If you weigh one of our umbrellas against an imported umbrella, there could be two or three pounds difference. It's because ours is heftier and has more quality built in."

Brickner is determined to uphold his family's legacy and commitment to quality, though. "It's something that you want to see keep going," he said. "You feel like you've put your whole life into a business and you want the business to succeed. You don't want it just to close up. That's what keeps me going."

Flickinger Glassworks is picture-perfect among its surroundings. Located on the historic warehouse docks of Red Hook, Brooklyn, it seems like just the place where one would find this kind of classic handiwork being done.

Flickinger Glassworks specializes in the art of glass bending for lighting, display counters, cabinetry, dishware, clock faces, or anything else that requires glass to be shaped, cast, etched, or enameled. "We will do everything from a little beveled piece of glass for Mrs. Smith's lighting fixture in Bay Ridge all the way to cast glass Art Deco panels for the Waldorf-Astoria Hotel and everything in between," said owner Charles Flickinger. Flickinger started his shop in 1985 after years under the apprenticeship of a few master craftsmen in New York City. His appreciation for these craftsmen shows with the miniature glass hall of fame exhibit—which profiles some of the city's best glass artisans—installed in the small shop at the front of the factory, which is open to the public.

At any given time, the workshop can have some 50 different jobs going at the same time. Inside the workshop are sheets upon sheets of glass of varying sizes, colors, and thicknesses, all of which are seemingly waiting patiently to be fashioned into something exquisite. Flickinger and his staff use techniques that have changed very little since they were perfected in Europe in the 18th century. The process starts with a cut flat sheet of glass, which is heated slightly to prevent shock. Next, it is placed onto a concave steel mold, which is akin to taking a sheet of paper and placing it on top of a bowl. The molds are either designed for the specific project or pulled from the company's 6,000-piece in-house mold collection, some of which date back to the 1830s. The glass and mold are placed into an oven with a temperature of around 1,200 degrees. Once inside, the pair spins much like a plate of food in a microwave oven. As the heat causes the glass to become more malleable, gravity and centrifugal force ease the glass into the mold. After it takes the desired shape, the glass is removed and put into the annealer, which is essentially a large metal box that slowly cools the piece overnight to avoid shock and breakage.

Larger pieces, like a glass display counter front, require a slightly different process. The glass and mold are put into the oven, and then a worker pokes a steel rod through a hole and carefully pushes the glass into the mold, finessing and coaxing it. This is a hard skill, but one that the craftsmen at Flickinger do with ease every day.

This kind of craftsmanship is one of the reasons Flickinger has a clientele list any manufacturer would envy—names like Polo Ralph Lauren, Museum of Modern Art, Ohio State Capitol, Macy's, Saks Fifth Avenue, architect I. M. Pei, Sotheby's, and New York Botanical Garden.

But perhaps the company's best-known work is seen by tens of thousands of people every day—the famed clock in the center of Grand Central Terminal, which Flickinger restored during the major renovation in the 1990s. The company also restored dozens of the terminal's unique lighting fixtures. "Grand Central was very satisfying from a glass standpoint, but also there was a lot of other very fine artisan work going on there and to see it all come together was a real treat," said Flickinger.

A more recent project was the Booth Theatre in Times Square, where the company replicated original etched glass light shades. The project was a challenge, but also a chance for Flickinger to learn and have fun. "I think that's what sets this company apart. I have to speak very quietly because my bookkeeper is in the office, but we really do not care that much if we make money. Sure, we have to stay in business, but on the other hand, you have to be challenged. You have to stretch the technology. I look forward to coming into work regardless of what is going to be on my plate for that day, and I've been doing it now for 26 years," he said.

FLICKINGER GLASSWORKS

Established in 1985

204 Van Dyke Street, Pier 41
Red Hook, Brooklyn
www.flickingerglassworks.com
718-875-1531
Subway: F or G train to Carroll Street
Open Monday–Friday:
9:00 a.m. to 5:00 p.m.

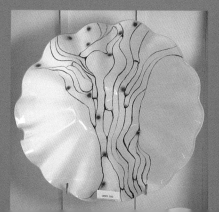

HOW-CAM.6cv
BROOKLYN, N.Y
CONTENTS 26 FL. OZ
- REGISTERED -

BRENTWOOD
BEVERAGE. CO.
BRENTWOOD, L.I

Canarsie
11236
BROOKLYN

Gone are the days of the milkman, bread truck, and seltzerman. Wait, scratch that. Seltzermen, who harken back to the days of cold water flats and soda fountains on every corner, are still making their rounds. Thankfully, there are still a few families and restaurants who appreciate the difference between seltzer made by a corporate conglomerate and the real stuff made simply with New York City tap water and hand-filled in classic glass seltzer bottles.

Gomberg Seltzer Works is to thank for the fact that this antiquated yet beloved part of New York City culture still exists. "We're the only ones left in the city," said third-generation owner Kenny Gomberg, who makes and bottles the seltzer himself. Located in a rather bland commercial section of Canarsie, Brooklyn, Gomberg—along with his brother-in-law, Irv Resnick—operates without fanfare, keeping authentic seltzer in the city in which it became famous.

Covering much of the city and even parts of New Jersey and Connecticut, independent seltzermen bring their bottles to Gomberg for filling and the occasional repair. Part of the appeal is that the company uses original bottles from the heyday of the seltzer industry. These thick and heavy glass bottles are often etched or printed with delightful logos of seltzer companies long gone. Many bottles are of the classic blue glass variety, hand-blown in Czechoslovakia. Upon walking into the Gomberg Seltzer Works bottling plant, the first thing one sees is stacks upon stacks of these vintage bottle beauties in antique wooden crates waiting to be filled.

According to Gomberg, his company's seltzer is far superior to any store-bought brands. "It's not even seltzer. It's out of a plastic bottle, and once you open that cap all the pressure goes out so it doesn't have much bite. Good seltzer should hurt when it's going down your throat," he said.

Making and bottling seltzer is not a streamlined, automated process, but rather an exercise in ingenuity and creativity. Gomberg uses the same machinery that seltzer makers used decades ago. Built in 1910 and imported from London, these rare and obsolete Barnett and Foster filler machines require a lot of care and maintenance. Out of sheer necessity, Gomberg has learned to repair the machines himself, often cannibalizing old machines and even making replacement parts from scratch.

When the machines are running smoothly, making seltzer begins with good old-fashioned New York City tap water, which is often underappreciated when it comes to municipal water. Piped in from upstate, it is considered some of the best public water in the country. Still, Gomberg Seltzer Works filters it three times. Next, the water is run through a refrigeration system called a "chiller," cooling it down to 43 degrees. From there, the water is drawn into a "carbonator," where it is mixed with CO_2 gas. Next, empty bottles are placed on a carousel-like feeder inside the siphon filler machine, where they are filled with seltzer using 60 pounds of pressure.

Gomberg Seltzer Works has been located at the same spot since 1953, when Gomberg's grandparents, Mo and Ester Gomberg, opened the business. Back then seltzer was so popular that they delivered it themselves by truck. Due to the high demand, whole routes would be a single block. Later their son, Pacey, took over, and then eventually passed the reins to Kenny. Today, deliveries are made to the elderly, who remember it from their youth, and a few restaurants who appreciate authenticity. Keeping with its old-fashioned ways, Gomberg Seltzer Works has no website and does not advertise. Still, business is brisk, with the company often filling more than 3,500 bottles a week.

According to Gomberg, the company is still being discovered for the first time by old-timers. "It is funny—there are people who find us, call us up, and just want to share stories from their past. They don't necessarily want the product; they just want to talk about it. Sometimes I feel like a therapist listening to their ramblings about the old times," he said, laughing.

GOMBERG SELTZER WORKS

Established in 1953

855 East 92nd Street, Carnasie, Brooklyn
718-257-9369
Bus: B17 to Remsen Avenue
Open Monday–Friday:
7:00 a.m. to 4:00 p.m.

THE GRAND PROSPECT HALL

Established in 1892

263 Prospect Avenue, Park Slope, Brooklyn
www.grandprospect.com 718-788-0777
Subway: D, N, or R train to Prospect Avenue
Open daily from 10:00 a.m. to 6:00 p.m.

It is one of the last Victorian-era ballrooms and vaudeville music halls left in America and it almost didn't make it into the 21st century. But now, thanks to some loving caretakers, The Grand Prospect Hall is ready for its close-up.

Located in Park Slope, Brooklyn, The Grand Prospect Hall is like a Fabergé egg, for its tasteful but plain exterior gives little hint of the opulent decor inside. The hall's Modern French Renaissance decor was inspired by the Palace of Versailles. Throughout it are bright color schemes reminiscent of the Victorian Age, including gold leaf, carved fruits, flowers, and other adornments. At four stories and 140,000 square feet, it houses 16 different rooms, each with its own purpose and theme. But the centerpiece of the hall is the Grand Ballroom, a two-tiered horseshoe-shaped room that holds up to 2,000 people.

The Grand Prospect Hall was rebuilt in 1900 after the original building burned down. Builders were determined to create a more opulent and extravagant replacement that would mirror the gilded mansions owned by the rich families of Park Slope, which was known at the time as Brooklyn's Gold Coast. The Grand Prospect Hall was at the time the tallest building in Brooklyn. It was also the first electrified commercial building in Brooklyn, and the first to be equipped with a French birdcage elevator.

Once open for business, the hall quickly took to its purpose of being a community center for cultural and political events. William Randolph Hearst and William Jennings Bryan both held rallies here while running for office. And in 1914, the Women's Suffrage Party began its national campaign here.

The hall was mostly known for its entertainment, though. Movies, dances, operas, and vaudeville shows were popular for years. The likes of Mae West, Bob Hope, Ginger Rogers, and Fred Astaire have performed here. Lena Horne got her professional start here as a teenager. Even Al Capone was said to have enjoyed going to the opera here. For a time, The Grand Prospect Hall was even an early movie studio; the Crescent Motion Picture Company used part of the building as its headquarters, making and showing silent films here.

During Prohibition, the hall created speakeasies. In fact, peepholes from that era still exist in the bar area.

As the years went by, the hall started to fall into disrepair and for a time the owners had to resort to hosting boxing matches, bingo, and flea markets to keep the building afloat. They even began selling off irreplaceable fixtures as business continued to dwindle. It didn't help matters when the Prospect Expressway sliced the neighborhood in half in the late 1950s.

...ER COVER SOCIET...

at PROSPECT HALL

263

263-273 Prospect Ave. Broo...

...VEDI 2 Ottob...

Alle ore 8 p.m.

...osa Serata Artistica in onore del Signo...

...LIO MOREL...

...dramma in 3 atti di LELIO MORELL...

...SVENTURAT...

Protagonisti:

Prospect Hall

Then, in 1981, The Grand Prospect Hall got a new beginning. Michael Halkias and his wife, Alice, purchased the building, becoming only the third owners in its 120-year history. They spent the next 30 years restoring the place before reopening it to the public. The restoration revealed several forgotten treasures, like small whimsical figurines painted on the oak panels. One is a caricature of President Theodore Roosevelt, who might not be too pleased with the illustration considering his rump is painted facing forward.

The restoration was only the beginning. Michael and Alice Halkias spent the next several years tracking down the fixtures previous owners had sold off. It has all been worth it, for the federal government recognized their work and dedication when it placed The Grand Prospect Hall on the National Registry of Historic Places in 1999.

Hollywood has also noticed The Grand Prospect Hall, using it as a backdrop for several movies, model shoots, commercials, and music videos. *The Cotton Club*, *The Royal Tenenbaums*, and *Prizzi's Honor* were all filmed here, as well as television show *Gossip Girl*.

Today, the hall is back and better than ever. During a busy week, it can host 18 to 25 events, including office parties, balls, dance competitions, and anniversaries. Not surprisingly, the hall hosts a lot of weddings. "The brides leave feeling that this is a dream-come-true building," said Alice Halkias. "I just got a call from a bride who got married here 25 years ago, and she said people are still talking about the wedding." And the future continues to look bright for this regal yet still relevant ballroom. Plans are underway to build a connecting hotel next door, which should keep the owners busy for many years to come.

"It's work, but that's not how we look at things. There's responsibility and duty, but it just so happens that we enjoy doing it. We could very well be somewhere else, on a mountain or a beach, but our commitment to this place is total," said Michael Halkias.

In Brooklyn, one can go horseback riding right into living history. This is thanks in part to Kensington Stables, a horse-back riding academy located near Prospect Park.

Kensington offers bridle path rides in Prospect Park for less than $40, and pony rides for kids for just a few dollars. Along with the stables, the paths are the last remnants of the time when horses were the dominant mode of transportation. In Brooklyn, hundreds of horses were stabled around Prospect Park, which itself was designed as if traveling by horse would never go out of style. "When Prospect Park was set up, there were riding academies at every intersection of the park and all the way down Ocean Parkway that all fed into the bridle path system," said Walker Blankinship, president of Kensington Stables.

The history of Kensington Stables began in 1917 when a private riding school was built on nearby Caton Place. The stable that Kensington occupies was built in 1930 as an extension to the academy. Blankinship, who was already boarding his own horses there, bought the business in 1993.

Kensington provides riding lessons for every age and skill level. According to Blankinship, one of the most important lessons to learn about riding is an understanding between the rider and the horse. "It is about having a partnership. You have to know every horse has its own personality and you have to help it along and what you're asking it for has to be fair. People think the horse just carries you along. You're an interactive backpack; you have to help the horse. It's your job to keep yourself in balance with what it's doing," he said.

The stable also on occasion provides horses for movie productions and fashion shoots. The stable provided horses for a music video for Alanis Morissette's song "Hand in My Pocket" and Tom Hanks's film *Extremely Loud and Incredibly Close*, among others. The many fashion shoots have provided Blankinship with a few chuckles. "They always want the sun, the moon, and the stars, like having the horse completely loose, running alone. A horse completely loose in Prospect Park. This is still the city. It doesn't work that way," he said.

On the outside, Kensington Stables looks like any other horse stable in America, albeit in the middle of Brooklyn. It is in an area that cannot quite decide if it is a residential or commercial neighborhood. Heading out for a ride in Prospect Park, horses share the road with cabbies and livery cabs driving to Manhattan. Like all other New Yorkers, the horses are oblivious to the hustle-and-bustle of the street, trotting along with as much confidence as any other local.

The stables are no-frills, but serve their purpose. There are no complaints from the horses though, for in some cases the stalls are roomier than a typical nearby studio apartment. Right upon entering the stables one can see that the horses are well taken care of—their shimmering coats are quite a contrast to their utilitarian surroundings. The horses are lively and playful with their caretakers, tussling the workers' hair or playing with them while they clean the stables.

Owning a horse stable in modern-day New York City does bring its own unique challenges, though. "We're basically a very isolated equine community. You don't have another horse farm next door who can lend you a hand. Our hay farmer is actually upstate 200 miles. It's very hard to find a farmer willing to drive into New York City to bring you supplies and to take the manure away," said Blankinship.

Even with the challenges, Blankinship knows he is providing a much-needed service to the city that is fun not only for the horses but also for New Yorkers. It is an important link between the past and present. One of the school trips Kensington frequently hosts illustrates this fact. "A boy from Brownsville came here and did not actually believe that horses were real," said Blankinship. "He thought they were Hollywood special effects that someone had created. He never realized that you could reach out and touch a living animal that was indeed a horse."

KENSINGTON STABLES

Established in 1993

51 Caton Place, Prospect Park, Brooklyn
www.kensingtonstables.com
718-972-4588
Subway: F or G train to
Fort Hamilton Parkway
Open daily from 10:00 a.m. to sunset

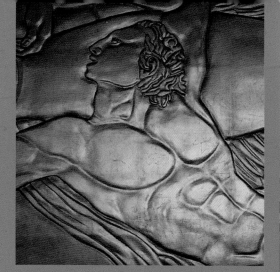

KODIAK STUDIOS

Established in 1995

168 Seventh Street, Suite 2B, Gowanus, Brooklyn
www.kodiakstudios.com 718-769-5399
Subway: F or G train to Fourth Avenue
Open by appointment only

If you have ever been to a local historical society, roadside stop, or museum in America, you have seen them: those life-sized human figures depicting some kind of historical event. Over the years, various institutions have stepped up their game, not merely using store mannequins dressed in period costumes, but commissioning incredibly lifelike installations.

This is where Kodiak Studios in Gowanus, Brooklyn, comes in. It is one of just a handful of artisan studios in the country creating these one-of-a-kind works of art. Owner Alex Tisch and his small team of artisans create hyperrealistic exhibit figures, which are used in museums and trade shows across the country. "I always consider my pieces the cherry on the cake," said Tisch. "Once the environment or diorama is built, my figures kind of cozy up to the exhibit and seal the deal on telling the story."

Tisch mastered life form sculpting at the Pratt Institute. Then, after apprenticing for a few years, he broke out on his own in 1995 to start Kodiak Studios. His figures are so detailed and well conceived that they sometimes startle museumgoers. The tiny details are so well executed that pores on the skin are visible and skin tones fluctuate over the entire body.

According to Tisch, this attention to detail is necessary. "Human beings have a tremendous emotional reaction to incredible detail and realism," he said. "If there are human eyes that are looking back at them in an exhibit, they just feel drawn in."

Kodiak Studios achieves such stunning detail through the process of "life casting," which is literally making a mold out of a real person. The process begins with auditions. Once a model is chosen and positioned in the desired pose, plaster medical bandages are wrapped around the person in three separate sections. Once dry, the molds are carefully removed from the model. Next, they are reassembled and a lightweight composite material is injected into the mold. Once this material hardens, the mold is removed to reveal the newly created figure. It is then sanded, painted, and clothed, and additional detail—like hair and glass eyes—are added. "When a piece is done, it looks like it was born and not made," said Tisch.

Through the years Kodiak Studios has created a wide range of figures, including astronauts, cowboys and Indians, portraits of historical people, presidents, and even dinosaurs. (As you might imagine, dinosaurs are far more difficult to cast.) The studio's work has been included in exhibits at the Museum of Natural History in New York, the Green Bay Packers Hall of Fame, the California Trails Museum, and the Miami Metro Zoo.

Although the work that Kodiak Studios does is extremely complicated and time-consuming, Tisch said the reward for all of its hard work is the reaction the figures sometimes get from clients. "It's really a lot of fun when you can produce work for someone and you send them to tears or they just hug you. You don't get that a lot in business," he said.

PAPER DRAGON BOOKS

Established in 2006

330 Morgan Avenue, No. 301, Williamsburg, Brooklyn
www.paperdragonbooks.com
646-633-7179
Subway: L train to Graham Avenue
Open by appointment only

In this ephemeral world of e-mail, e-books, and texting, there is comfort knowing that the printed word—meaning words printed on actual paper—is still cherished. Paper Dragon Books is such a place; it is a classic bookbinder that uses traditional techniques while continually elevating bookbinding as an art form. "We do basically anything that has sheets of paper hand-stitched along one side and has a handmade cover on it," said owner Gavin Dovey.

A native Brit, Dovey came to the United States in 2003, having mastered the craft of bookbinding at the London College of Printing, United Kingdom. After teaching classes at the Center for Book Arts, New York, he decided to open Paper Dragon Books in 2006. Located in a renovated warehouse, Paper Dragon Books is perfectly suited for the open loft-like space. Work is done on large tables filled with classic old-world tools, with raw materials like goatskin, gold leaf, and parchment waiting to the side to be made into something unforgettable.

The company's work is all done in-house by Dovey and his employees, including Ramon Perdomo, a skilled veteran bookbinder. Projects include both book restorations and full bookbinding from scratch. It also makes custom archival boxes to house books and other cherished items. Binding projects range from dozens of presentational copies of a corporation's annual report to a newlywed's wedding album. Clients range from storied institutions like the Morgan Library and Museum to the weekend book collector.

When it comes to traditional bookbinding, a bookbinder begins with what are called "signatures." These are essentially folds of paper that are sewn together through the middle. Next, the book is "backed," meaning the newly created spine is glued up, rounded, and the edges are trimmed. The book cover is then mounted onto the pages and the book is complete.

The amount of time put into a book can vary wildly. A simple project takes two days, while larger projects take two weeks—or longer. "I could agonize over designing something really complicated and labor-intensive for even two years," said Dovey. Covers can range from something as simple as gray cloth to one-of-a-kind pieces made of leather. This is where Dovey's unique talents really come out. For instance, one regular client collects signed first editions of books. He commissions Dovey to construct clamshell archival boxes for each book. Looking much like a book itself, Dovey decorates each box with illustrations of pivotal scenes from the book. In many cases, Dovey's wildly creative designs are more intriguing than the actual book cover. Incredibly, he uses pieces of leather much like a wood veneer. He fuses together a mosaic of pieces that are melded together to create a seamless image.

How does Dovey feel about the future of bookbinding as the world embarks on the digital age? He remains optimistic. "As long as things are collectible and people need that tangible connection with something that they hold in their hands, there will be a need. To me, that's kind of like asking why anyone would have art when we have photography or computers," he said.

You can't miss Pastosa Ravioli's flagship store in Bensonhurst, Brooklyn. Its technicolor red and white storefront is a welcoming visual diversion from a rather bland section of New Utrecht Avenue. Its interior does not disappoint either, for there is a cornucopia of Italian food delights. It is a place that makes shopping a joy and where people from the neighborhood often stop by just to chat.

Pastosa Ravioli's name is a bit of a misnomer. *Pastosa* in Italian means "plethora or variety of pasta," which the shop indeed has—including 35 different varieties of ravioli alone. This is anything but just a ravioli shop, though. It is an Italian supermarket without the big-box chain store feel and with all the sights and smells of Grandma's kitchen. "When you go to one of these one-stop-shop places, you're a number. We pride ourselves on the fact that we know 90 percent of our customers by name; we know their mothers, their fathers, their children," said co-owner Anthony Ajello.

Ajello's grandfather, also named Anthony Ajello, founded Pastosa Ravioli in 1967. "It started over a bottle of scotch," he said. "Grandfather was sitting in the backyard with a friend of his and they were playing cards and drinking. My grandmother had just made an Italian meal for them and he decided that he wanted to go into the ravioli business." Already a ricotta salesman for Polly O, he knew there was a need for more artisanal old-world pasta and ravioli in New York City. His son, Michael, later joined the business, as well as a business partner, Tony Postiglione. Now, more than 40 years later, his grandsons, Anthony and Joseph Ajello, along with their sister, Jacqueline, run the business. It is a pasta empire that now includes 11 stores in Staten Island, Brooklyn, Queens, Long Island, the Bronx, and New Jersey.

The stores offer just about any kind of Italian food or delicacy one can think of—pasta, sauces, imported ingredients, and even prepared meals like chicken cutlet parmesan, grilled vegetables, and veal cutlet. Daily selections bursting with color look and smell fresh in their refrigerated cabinets. Because much of the food is made in-house in a factory behind the shop, prices are competitive with big-box supermarkets.

Pastosa Ravioli also imports many items directly from Italy, including cheeses, aged meats, and sausages. "We even import our tomatoes," said Ajello. "We've been buying tomatoes in Italy from the same people for more than 40 years." Pastosa uses the tomatoes in its own brand of homemade sauces, including marinara, vodka, and tomato cream and basil sauce. The shop even makes mozzarella daily. "Mozzarella should be eaten the day it is made. Our customers know there's a lot of ways to mishandle the mozzarella and this is something that's been in my family for generations so we're keeping that tradition alive," said Ajello.

It is the pasta that is the company's crowning achievement, though. The linguine, rigatoni, and fettuccine at Pastosa are so good that a few fine restaurants are known to pass the pasta off as their own "special brand." The company's pastas are made daily in its special pasta room with machines imported from Italy. Ravioli—with fillings like ricotta cheese, meat, lobster, spinach, salmon, truffles, and even pumpkin—is the best seller. Pastosa can make upwards of 5,000 raviolis in an hour. "My grandfather always said if going to work is a battlefield then you're in the wrong business. We enjoy what we do and there's a deep, deep sense of family pride," said Ajello.

PASTOSA RAVIOLI

Established in 1967

7425 New Utrecht Avenue
Bensonhurst, Brooklyn
www.pastosa.com 718-236-9615
Subway: D train to 79th Street
Open Monday–Saturday:
8:30 a.m. to 6:30 p.m.
Sunday: 8:30 a.m. to 3:00 p.m.
Check website for information
about other store locations in Brooklyn,
Queens, the Bronx, Staten Island,
Long Island, and New Jersey.

TEDDY'S BAR AND GRILL

Established in 1887

96 Berry Street, Williamsburg, Brooklyn
www.teddyswilliamsburg.com
718-384-9787
Subway: L train to Bedford Avenue
Open Sunday–Thursday:
11:30 a.m. to 1:00 a.m.
Friday–Saturday:
11:30 a.m. to 3:00 a.m.

In a short time, Williamsburg, Brooklyn, has gone from a rough-and-tumble working-class neighborhood to a hip, trendy hot spot. Through it all, there has been a quaint neighborhood bar quietly hanging on through the area's transformations, proving a business does not have to be young to be hip.

Teddy's Bar and Grill sits on a quiet residential street, which is fitting since it radiates neighborliness and has long been a staple in the community. "People would come down to bars like this, and that would be their living room. That was the culture of this neighborhood originally, and this bar originally. That idea in a new form is what we seek to have here," said co-owner Lee Ornati.

The clientele is a cross-section of, well, everybody, and all seem pleased to have each other's company. "We still have our traditional blue-collar working-class community that built New York side-by-side coexisting with the whole new, artistic, youth-oriented community," said co-owner Felice Kirby.

Teddy's is an authentic Victorian-era bar and is one of only a few left in the city. Built in 1887, much of its interior is original. The tin ceilings and tiny tiles, standard in many era bars like this, have been lovingly cared for, and the main room still has its ornate hand-carved wood

hutch behind the bar. Art from local artists adorns the wall, along with yellowed photographs of past patrons. Shortly after the bar was built, the Peter Doelger Brewery Company franchised the business, supplying it with its own beer. Although the brewing company has closed its doors, remnants of that time still exist, including the centerpiece of the bar's fixtures: a beautiful stained glass window with the words "Peter Doelger's Extra Beer." It is one of the oldest pieces of original advertising still used in a New York City establishment.

When the current owners—Lee Ornati and Felice and Glenn Kirby—took over a few years ago, they renovated the place but were careful to keep much of it the same. They did make one major change, though. Indoor plumbing was added in the 1940s, but the bathroom was hastily installed in—of all places—the stage area in the center of the bar. During renovations, the bathrooms were moved to a more appropriate place, giving the bar its stage back.

The stained glass Doelger window was given special treatment. The owners shipped it back to the original glass factory in Germany where it was created. Craftsmen there were able to give it a truer restoration than could be done in America, for some of the lead content required to make the glass is no longer allowed to be used in this country.

HARVEST
SEASON -
TIME TO
DRINK NEW
YORK STATE
WINE!

*Drink local! It's
good for us all!*

FIRST BREW PRIZE

CONTAINS LESS THAN ½ OF 1% ALCOHOL BY VOLUME

Peter Doelger

BREWING CO. INC.

NEW YORK

N.Y.—L—77

ESTABLISHED 1859

WINE...

Beautiful Reds
*NYS   *Cal* Pinot Noir
*Pinot Noir   *Red Zin
*Cab Franc   *French
                *Bordeaux
*Spanish   *Italian
*Malbec   *Chianti
*Merlot   *Salice Salentino
*Tempranilla   *Barolo (bottle only)

PETER DOELGER'S EXTRA BEER

Also restored was the original copper and wood front facade. Before the renovation, the deterioration was so bad that during rainy days people would sit in the bar with umbrellas. Unfortunately, just 10 months after the restoration two cars jumped the curb, crashing right through the bar. The front had to be completely reconstructed yet again.

This particular bar also played an interesting part in New York City history. In the 1920s, it was a meeting place for the notorious Tammany Hall political machine. Many secret backroom deals were said to have happened over mugs of beer. And like any bar around this long, it became a speakeasy during Prohibition. Proof of its dubious past still exists in the form of frosted glass panes, which were part of a series of sliding glass doors. The doors were used to conceal the bar area so Teddy's looked as if it was only a restaurant.

Teddy's has a few other claims to fame as well. Mae West—a cousin to one of the Doelgers—lived upstairs while she was getting her start in New York. Scenes from the 1990 movie *Kings of New York* were shot here, as were numerous fashion shoots and television shows.

In addition to its rich history, the food at Teddy's also keeps people coming back day after day. Part of the menu is traditional American bar food, but the owners also like to draw inspiration from international bar food traditions as well. "We try to take those ideas and infuse them with American spirit and the best ingredients we can find," said Ornati. The bar also takes pride in its wine list, offering about 20 labels, including a few from New York State vineyards.

Through it all, Teddy's continues to be a place that serves the community. "Teddy's opens itself up proudly as a meeting place, a discussion place for the issues that concern our new neighbors," said Kirby. "It is a place to build community, hold fund-raisers, and discuss the issues." Now that it has its stage back, it also offers live music. Just about any musical genre is offered here—world music, blues, and jazz, in particular—and performances are scheduled several nights a week. Customers can call for more information about these events. Considering the good music, good food, and all-around good atmosphere, it is no surprise that Teddy's has stood the test of time and is now a vital part of the new Williamsburg culture.

RUSS & DAUGHT[ERS]
APPETIZERS

John's

RESTAURANT PIZZA

E.O.Bi[g]

THE CITY

BROOKLYN
STABLES

TINY D[

ONIEA[

GRAND ST[

Lexington
Candy Shop

LUNCHEONETTE

MANHATTAN

THE BITTER END

Established in 1961

147 Bleecker Street, Greenwich Village, Manhattan
www.bitterend.com 212-673-7030
Subway: B, D, F, or M train to Broadway–Lafayette Street
Open Sunday–Thursday: 7:30 p.m. to 2:00 a.m.
Friday–Saturday: 7:30 p.m. to 4:00 a.m.

Where else but New York City could there be a place where the likes of Bob Dylan and Bill Cosby both honed their skills before hitting it big? This has always been the essence of The Bitter End—the oldest rock club in New York City—a spot where up-and-coming artists of all kinds have found a nurturing place in this often-unforgiving city.

The formula is simple. "It is an intimate setting. We cater to musicians and musical people and that's really all it is. No screens, no sports, no models walking down runways. It's very basic, it's music," said Ken Gorka, owner and manager of the club. Basic, perhaps, but it is also amazing, for The Bitter End has managed to stay this way close to 50 years, through all the trends, fads, and fickleness of the entertainment business.

At first glance, The Bitter End looks like a standard live performance club. There is a small stage in the center of the room with a red brick background, which is surrounded by tables and chairs for a couple hundred people. Like any other music club, its walls are covered with posters, album covers, and photographs of past performers. But at The Bitter End, these past performers are legends of the entertainment world—names like George Carlin, Linda Ronstadt, Jay Leno, Kris Kristofferson, Lady Gaga, and Sarah McLachlan. In fact, the Rock and Roll Hall of Fame has even acquired a few of the club's items for its museum, including an old wooden phone booth that was a fixture at the club for decades.

The Bitter End is part of the long musical tradition of Bleecker Street in Greenwich Village. This is the street where artists can experiment, learn the way of the business, and get noticed. The club was named for its location on Bleecker, because it was at the end of the street, thus the "bitter end" of all that was musical and progressive. Now, just a few clubs remain from the street's 1960s heyday, and The Bitter End is the granddaddy of them all.

The club opened in 1961, when owner Fred Weintraub and manager Paul Colby turned what was then a sleepy coffeehouse into an entertainment hub. Eventually, Paul Colby took ownership; now in his 90s, he still helps make sure new artists get their shot on stage. "The Bitter End was one of the most important clubs for me as I made my steps to professional musicianship," said singer John Sebastian. When Sebastian branched out as a solo artist after the end of his band The Loving Spoonful, the first thing he did was talk to Paul Colby about the possibility of opening for another band.

The club has always been a place where both new artists and superstars alike enjoyed performing, especially now

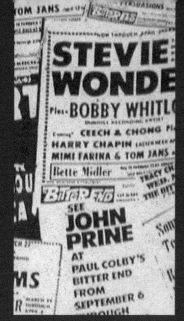

STEVIE WONDER
Plus BOBBY WHITLOCK
CEECH & CHONG
HARRY CHAPIN
MIMI FARINA & TOM JANS
Bette Midler

SEE
JOHN PRINE
AT
PAUL COLBY'S
BITTER END
FROM
SEPTEMBER 6

THE BITTER END

TERRA BLUES

Paul Colby's
THE BITTER END

Etta James
Billy Joel
Stevie Wonder
Bob Dylan
Bill Cosby
Jerry Jeff Walker
Woody Allen
Linda Ronstadt
Jackson Browne

August 13

SANDRA BERNHARD

9pm
$7

that its intimate setting is a rarity in this era of mega arenas and performing arts centers. Many of these new artists quickly became superstars, one of which was James Taylor. "I remember the first time I ever saw James Taylor here. I think he had 20 people in the audience," said Gorka. "So you could imagine for James Taylor to have 20 people, how long ago that was." Two other unknowns who wowed audiences: Bette Midler and Barry Manilow, who sometimes played here together.

One of The Bitter End's high points was in the mid-1960s, when the club hosted Tuesday night folk hootenannies. These live shows helped foster the modern folk movement. Musicians like Arlo Guthrie, Joan Baez, and Peter, Paul and Mary were just some of the acts that performed at the club in those days. Peter, Paul and Mary even recorded a live album there, and their first album cover features them on stage at the club.

Of all the musical legends to walk through the door, though, Bob Dylan is the one that sticks out. He has been coming to the club for years, not only to perform but also to check out new music. According to Gorka, Dylan often sneaks in to watch other performers and no one knows he is there. In fact, one of Gorka's fondest memories of the performer was when he came in to see John Prime perform. Prime noticed Dylan in the audience and invited him on stage to play harmonica. He agreed, played one song, and then left the club. Gorka was standing next to a couple

at the time and overheard their conversation. "The man looked at the woman and said, 'Isn't that funny? That guy really did look like Bob Dylan,'" said Gorka, laughing. The couple couldn't comprehend that Bob Dylan was actually in the club.

In addition to music, The Bitter End was also a trailblazer for stand-up comedy. It was one of the first incarnations of the modern-day comedy club, complete with the brick wall background behind the stage, which has inspired countless copycats. Stand-up comics Cheech and Chong, Billy Crystal, Albert Brooks, and Joan Rivers have all performed at the club. Combination comedy and music shows were standard fare at The Bitter End for years. There actually was a time when singer Carly Simon and her sisters would open for comedians Bill Cosby and Woody Allen.

The Bitter End continues its tradition of helping musicians in any way it can, which includes the club's "door deal policy"—one of the last in the city. The cover charges don't go to the club, but rather straight to the musicians' pockets, giving struggling artists a financial boost. Once they hit it big, many of these musicians come back to try out new material or take a break from the big venues. A few who have recently returned are Joss Stone, Lady Gaga, and Neil Diamond. Today, The Bitter End is as relevant as ever, putting on shows nightly, sometimes six acts in a row, and helping to continue its legacy as *the* place to hear new music in New York.

CAFFE REGGIO

Established in 1921

119 MacDougal Street, Greenwich Village, Manhattan
www.caffereggio.com 212-475-9557
Subway: A, C, E, B, D, F, or M train to
West Fourth Street
Open Monday–Thursday:
8:00 a.m. to 3:00 a.m.
Friday–Saturday: 8:00 a.m. to 4:30 a.m.
Sunday: 9:00 a.m. to 3:00 a.m.

In New York City, not to mention the rest of America, café society has pretty much surrendered itself to the corporate coffeehouse. Starbucks, Dunkin' Donuts—you name it—coffee now has a corporate philosophy. That is too bad, for there is nothing like the homegrown atmosphere of a one-of-a-kind café that has managed to stick around for decades.

Proof of this is Caffe Reggio on MacDougal Street in the heart of Greenwich Village. It is one of those places just begging you to wile the day away in its surroundings with a good book and cup of coffee. Caffe Reggio is the oldest original café in the neighborhood and it wears its patina well, looking much the same as it did when it opened in the 1920s. It exudes the feeling of an Italian café, a crowded space with petite tables and cute waitresses weaving between them to fill orders. "You cannot duplicate this atmosphere with a sort of prepackaged thing like a Starbucks," said manager Tobia Buggiani. "This place has been around forever, and it really has its own look and feel. It's unique, it's warm, and it's authentic."

Caffe Reggio was opened in 1927 by Italian immigrant Domenico Parisi, who initially put a barber's shop in the space, but had always dreamed of opening a café. At the time, coffeehouses were few and far between. In fact, Caffe Reggio was the first Italian coffeehouse in the United States and actually helped usher in the country's love for gourmet coffee.

One of the first things Parisi did after opening the café was buy a cappuccino machine from Italy. It cost $1,000—his entire life savings—and was the first of its kind in America. "There are old articles from the '20s and '30s about people coming into Greenwich Village to see this sort of curiosity," said Buggiani. "And then they would get served this incredible coffee that was so different from anything that had been in the United States prior to that." Amazingly, that very cappuccino machine is still at the café, prominently displayed in the main room. Though the coal-fired, custom-made machine still works, it was retired in the 1980s due to its value and tenure of service.

Parisi continued to serve his coffee until 1955, when married couple Niso and Hilda Cavallacci bought the shop from him. They took care of it until the 1970s, then passed it on to their son, Fabrizio, who is the current owner. Buggiani manages the day-to-day operations and, like a good classic mom-and-pop proprietor, he even lives upstairs. "I am a manager at the oldest café in New York City, which is something that I take a lot of pride in," he said. "A lot of

what I do is making sure that this place remains authentic and not just another sort of commercial place on MacDougal Street."

With each owner and caretaker, Caffe Reggio acquired more furnishings and decorations. These aren't just knick-knacks, though; they are exquisite original works of art. Many customers are unaware of the treasures that surround them. There are more than 80 pieces of artwork, including paintings, sculptures, and custom-made furniture. Some of the paintings date back to the Renaissance era. One painting is even attributed to the school of Caravaggio, one of the giants of the era, and was possibly painted by one of his students.

At one spot in the café, you can drink your coffee where royalty once sat. It is a dark wood bench originally owned by the Medicis, a prominent family who rose to power in Italy during the Renaissance. The family crest carved into the wood has been conspicuously taken out, which was the practice of the time when such items transferred ownership.

This eclectic blend of art is perfect for the eras Caffe Reggio has lived through. Like any true coffeehouse in Greenwich Village, it has been the backdrop for a multitude of trends, movements, and events. It was one of the intellectual hubs for the bohemian, beat, and folk movements. Some of the café's past customers include musician Bob Dylan and poet Jack Kerouac. Even Elvis Presley enjoyed a cup of joe here.

Hollywood has also noticed this legendary spot. Several movies have been shot here, including the original *Shaft*, *Next Stop Greenwich Village*, and *The Godfather Part II*. There's even a piece of movie history on the ceiling— a ceiling fan that was used as a prop in the movie *Casablanca*. It still works and is used in the summertime.

Regardless of all its interesting decor and history, people keep coming back to Caffe Reggio for the food and drinks. The café has an eclectic menu, serving everything from small pasta dishes, paninis, salads, and soups to a wide variety of pastries and cakes. The café tries to purchase most of its ingredients from historical and local vendors.

But it is the coffee that sets Caffe Reggio apart. It is a place for true coffee connoisseurs, and it serves all kinds— Americano, mocha, cappuccino, caffe latte, espresso, doppio espresso, and macchiato. "We are meticulous about the kind of coffee bean that we use," said Buggiani. "If you go to some of these chain coffee places, you get this horrifically burned, bitter coffee. An espresso bean should be well roasted, but it shouldn't be burned. That's what Caffe Reggio is constantly striving to do: provide the customer with a real coffee taste, not something you have to drown with syrups and sugars."

When people think of the neighborhood of Chelsea, they think art and fashion—but quilting? Thanks to a husband-and-wife team, many indeed do. Cathy Izzo and Dale Riehl's shop, The City Quilter, brings small-town America to an otherwise trendy area. But don't be fooled—quilting isn't just Granny's hobby anymore. In fact, many New Yorkers welcome the soothing craft as a break from the usual hustle-and-bustle of the city.

"When we say we own a quilt shop in New York City, people look at us a little funny," said Riehl. But, according to Izzo, it actually makes perfect sense. "This is the fabric capitol of the United States," she said. "Also, quilting is quite an art form, and this is the art capitol of the world."

Izzo and Riehl opened The City Quilter after growing tired of their day jobs. "For years, my husband and I were television producers who spent all our time at a computer, but there was nothing tangible at the end of the day. I wanted to be able to feel something I've made," said Izzo.

Now the shop is known locally, nationally, and internationally for all things quilting—fabric, sewing notions or tools, embroidery supplies, and more than 100 different quilting classes for varying skill levels. But what makes this place particularly special is its incredible supply of fabric bolts. There are more than 4,000 kinds in designs of every conceivable pattern and subject matter, along with handmade fabrics from as far away as Africa and Indonesia—all ready and waiting to become part of a new project. With this kind of eclectic selection, the shop also attracts non-quilting shoppers who sew dresses, curtains, bags, or other projects from its fabrics.

Much like knitting managed to do a few years ago, quilting is making a comeback, quickly finding a huge fan base in New York City. Not only is it calming—"Yoga for the lazy," as Izzo put it—quilting is also a nice diversion during a long commute or a way to wind down after work. And Izzo believes there is another good reason for this resurgence in quilting. "There is a generation or two that skipped over home economics and the domestic arts. They didn't ever learn how to sew even basic things. Those are the ones coming in thinking, 'It's good to know how to mend something, but it's also a lot of fun to make something from scratch.' Younger people are discovering that," she said.

Furthermore, The City Quilter and its classes help to bring a neighborly feel to a town that is often standoffish by attracting a wide variety of customers. "We have investment bankers, Broadway performers, lawyers, accountants—you name it," said Izzo.

Like any art form, quilting continues to change and evolve. Many people are unaware of just how intricate and abstract some quilts are in design. That's one of the reasons Izzo and Riehl opened an art gallery devoted solely to quilting right next door. One recent exhibit featured artist Noriko Endo from Japan. She used thousands upon thousands of confetti-size fabric pieces to re-create landscapes, much like Impressionist painters used broad strokes of paint. These and other wondrous creations at the gallery can go for thousands of dollars.

With the shop and gallery, Izzo and Riehl have a modest yet earnest goal: making people a little happier with an art form that has provided them with so much joy. "I think New York can sometimes be a very gray city, especially in the winter," said Izzo. "Then you walk into our store and there's this burst of Technicolor. We call it color therapy. It makes you feel happier and more alive."

THE CITY QUILTER

Established in 1997

133 West 25th Street
Chelsea, Manhattan
www.cityquilter.com
www.artquiltgallerynyc.com
212-807-0390
Subway: E, F, N, or 1 train
to 23rd Street
Open Tuesday–Friday:
11:00 a.m. to 7:00 p.m.
Saturday: 10:00 a.m. to 6:00 p.m.
Sunday: 11:00 a.m. to 5:00 p.m.

THE CITY QUILTER

Learn to Quilt Here!

C. O. BIGELOW

Established in 1838

414 Sixth Avenue, Greenwich Village, Manhattan
www.bigelowchemists.com 212-533-2700
Subway: A, B, C, D, E, F, or M train
to West Fourth Street
Open Monday–Friday: 7:30 a.m. to 9:00 p.m.
Saturday: 8:30 a.m. to 7:00 p.m.
Sunday: 8:30 a.m. to 5:30 p.m.

Before there were chain-store pharmacies, health care insurance, or even an abundance of doctors, many early Americans relied on the local apothecary. A cross between a pharmacy and a family physician, apothecaries treated minor illnesses like colds or rashes, often making medicine or compounds in-house. It was not unusual for apothecaries to even conduct an occasional surgery or assist a mother with childbirth.

Apothecaries for the most part have transformed into the modern pharmacy, but personal care and customer service did not necessarily follow. Luckily for New York City, the apothecary experience is still available (minus the childbirths and in-house surgeries, of course) at one of the last and oldest apothecaries in America—C. O. Bigelow. Company president and owner Ian Ginsberg said, "I think it's an experience that's been yanked from customers that never really wanted it taken away. Let's say you're not feeling well. You have the choice of going to a chain store where they'll say, 'Well, the cold stuff is over there,' or you can come here where our pharmacy clerks say, 'What's the matter? Tell me what's wrong,' and they'll assist you in picking the right medicine."

C. O. Bigelow takes customer service so seriously that almost all of its medicines—whether they're typically over-the-counter drugs or not—are behind the counter and out of reach of the customers. "We do that on purpose because we want that connection with the customer," said Ginsberg. "Frankly, that's what we're here for."

Over the decades, C. O. Bigelow has served a real cross section of old New York notables, including Mark Twain, Thomas Edison, Franklin and Eleanor Roosevelt, and Mae West. The shop still has many of their original pharmacy records. Peeking at Mae West's purchases could be rather interesting, but sorry, store policy forbids employees from revealing any information from customer records—even if the customer is dead.

The history of C. O. Bigelow goes back to 1838, when it was founded by Doctor Galen Hunter—just two doors down from its current location. It was passed from employer to employee until Clarence Otis Bigelow took over in 1880, renaming it after himself and building its current home in 1902. Over the years, the business again passed through employees' hands until William Ginsberg purchased it with his brother-in-law, Arthur Gross, in 1939. Several family members have worked at the shop, including Gross's sons, Steve and Jack, and Ginsberg's son, Jerry. It is Jerry's son, Ian Ginsberg, who is now running things.

Entering C. O. Bigelow's landmarked building is a rarified experience, for it is one of very few Victorian-era store interiors left in the city. The ornate interior is filled with beautiful decor and fixtures, like the original wood cabinets, which were specifically handcrafted for the shop. There are several ornate touches, like sculpted Bs on the ceiling and original brass gas lighting fixtures, which have been retrofitted for electricity. For a while, they could still work on gas and were used during the blackouts of 1965 and 1977, which made C. O. Bigelow one of very few businesses in the area able to remain open.

In the back of the C. O. Bigelow store is the heart of its business. There is a row of pharmacy attendants in blue coats eagerly waiting on customers. Behind them is a team of pharmacists, some of which have been with the company for almost 40 years.

Up until the 1980s, C. O. Bigelow also had a soda fountain luncheonette. "It was a gathering place, a kind of who's who of cool New York—customers included Ron Reagan Jr., John Belushi from *Saturday Night Live*, Mayor Ed Koch, and the New York Dolls, among others," said Ginsberg. Today, only the wall that was behind the wood soda fountain remains, but it has been wonderfully restored.

C. O. Bigelow is also famous for stocking hard-to-find health care and cosmetic items from around the world. "There are so many great products out there that get lost in the sea of plan-o-grams and chain stores," said Ginsberg. "I love brands that have a great story; they have to have a heritage." Examples include Email Diamant, a French toothpaste that causes teeth to appear whiter by coloring

the gums pinker. There is also Dr. Singha's Mustard Bath to "soothe aches and calm minds." And let us not forget Swiss Kriss, a 100-year-old herbal tea that works as a laxative. Just don't drink it during your morning commute.

Taking a page from its ancestors, C. O. Bigelow has recently reintroduced some of its Victorian-era products straight out of its original recipe books, including classic products like lip balms, soaps, and skin creams. According to Ginsberg, the company's recipe books are a fascinating read into how pharmacognosy has changed. "You see a lot of things that were made in suppository form and a lot of mouth rinses," he said. "We also did a lot of animal medicine in those days."

The company has also partnered with Limited Brands, which now sells the C. O. Bigelow product line through its Bath and Body Works stores.

As the years go by, C. O. Bigelow continues to find ways to enhance the customer experience at the store. And if its customers are any indication, it must be doing something right. "We see celebrities all the time," said Ginsberg. "You know these kinds of people probably don't run their own errands at the grocery store or dry cleaner, but the one thing they do is come to Bigelow's, which means there is something about this place that makes them want to come here and hang out. So when I see someone like Diane Von Furstenberg or Calvin Klein walking around the aisles with a basket of stuff, it kind of makes my day."

C.O. BIGELOW
PHARMACY
Estab.
1838.

PRESCRIPTIONS
COSMETICS
SURGICAL
SUPPLIES
HOME CARE
FREE DELIVERY
533-2700

orange

Ossimeᵉ Sempᵉ

WHITENESS & FRESHNESS
EMAIL
DIAMANT

WHITENESS & PURITY
EMAIL
DIAMANT

POTTER'S
POTTER'S
POTTER'S
POTTER'S
POTTER'S
POTTER'S
POTTER'S

ANTI-TACHES
DOUBLE ACTION

Formule
BICARBONATE
& FLUOR

ANTI STAIN
DUAL ACTION

DR. SINGHA'S THERAPEUTICS
Dr. Singha's
Soothing Purifying Relaxing
Mustard Bath
gentle herbal formula with Organic Powdered Mustard,
Wintergreen & Thyme

New York City, like the rest of America, has seen the mom-and-pop bookstore purged from its landscape, due in part to online sales, e-readers, and other 21st-century shifts in technology. But The Complete Traveller in Manhattan has managed to buck the trend by being extraordinary. Not only was it the first bookstore in the country to devote itself solely to travel-related books, it also is known worldwide for its unique inventory of antiquarian books.

It began with owner Arnold Greenberg and his wife, Harriet, in the 1970s. "We started in 1978 because we were writing travel guidebooks and needed someone to distribute the books into bookstores. The man who became our distributor had the idea of opening a travel bookstore with all modern guidebooks from everywhere," said Greenberg. "I liked the atmosphere of the store," added his wife, Harriet. "It was always busy and people were excited because they were going places."

When demand for new travel books began to wane, the Greenbergs changed gears, focusing on only vintage travel books. Today, along with having the most comprehensive inventory of travel-related books in New York City, the shop also has some 400 historic maps, a few non-travel first-edition collectibles, and a few vintage comic books.

Its inventory of Baedeker travel guides is quite possibly the largest collection in the world. First created by Karl Baedeker in the 1830s, these books about individual countries are regarded as the first modern versions of a travel guide, coming into vogue just as the steam engine opened up new possibilities for travel. Baedeker guidebooks are coveted for their honest and comprehensive reviews, along with their extremely detailed maps. In fact, military officers in some European countries were known to use Baedeker maps instead of their own. Today, a rare Baedeker guidebook in fine condition can sell for a few thousand dollars. The Complete Traveller is also well-known for its selection of WPA travel guides, put out by the Works Progress Administration during the Depression.

Why would you want an antique travel guide, which most likely has places and attractions—not to mention countries—that no longer exist? "Say you are going to take a trip to Rome," said store manager Mike Durell. "A place like that is so steeped in history that it would really be illuminating to find out what people were saying about it many years ago. You get information that you wouldn't get now." It is also interesting to see how opinions have changed over the course of history. "In British publications about places like Africa and the South Seas, there was a great deal of condescension toward native peoples," said Durell. "They were pretty much convinced they were the apogee of human perfection and that everybody else was lesser beings."

The Complete Traveller Bookstore also sees a lot of historians and writers who use the shop's books for research and plot locations. For example, one recent visitor to the bookstore was writing a book about Sigmund Freud. Freud mentioned a certain period of time when he came up with some theory, and he mentioned the name of the hotel where he was staying. "This guy wanted to see if that place really existed. We looked and we found the place for him," said Greenberg.

Does store manager Durell think that bookstores, like some of the places profiled in the books The Complete Traveller carries, are doomed to extinction? The answer is no. "There's something about being able to hold a book in your hands that gives you much more pride of ownership than digital letters on a screen," he said. "Also, nothing is going to replace the fun of browsing."

THE COMPLETE TRAVELLER

Established in 1978

199 Madison Avenue
Murray Hill, Manhattan
www.ctrarebooks.com
212-685-9007
Subway: 6 train to 33rd Street;
B, D, F, N, Q, R, V, or W train
to 34th Street
Open Monday–Friday:
9:30 a.m. to 6:30 p.m.
Saturday: 10:00 a.m. to 6:00 p.m.
Sunday: 12:00 p.m. to 5:00 p.m.

Remember stationery? You know, that stuff made for writing letters and notes? Before e-mail, Facebook, and Twitter, people actually put their thoughts to pen and paper. Now that exercise has seemingly gone the way of the dial telephone and telegraph. But fear not, you lovers of the handwritten word. On the Upper East Side, there is a shop that is still perfecting the fine art of letter writing: Dempsey & Carroll.

Dempsey & Carroll sits on Lexington Avenue near 75th Street, perfectly sandwiched between other well-heeled boutiques and shops. This tasteful and elegant shop's specialty is customized engraved stationery—be it letterhead, note cards, wedding announcements, or business cards—anything that makes a statement. In fact, everyone from former presidents to Oprah Winfrey has had stationery made by Dempsey & Carroll. The shop also carries a line of fountain pens and supplies, as well as leather desk accessories.

Dempsey & Carroll was founded in 1878 by master engraver John Dempsey and businessman George D. Carroll in New York's Union Square. At one point, the company employed some 100 staff members and even published books. As the industry died down, Dempsey & Carroll became one of very few stationery companies to survive in the city. Now, it is one of the last in the United States still making hand-engraved custom stationery. Today, Dempsey & Carroll is run by CEO Lauren Marrus, a marketing executive by trade who previously helped set up numerous Internet sites for big-name corporate clients.

"The great thing about personalized stationery is that it's built from the ground up," said former general manager Jonathan Key Arnold. "You're choosing your paper color, your ink color, your type face, so you can really make engraved stationery your own. It should reflect who you are and your personality." And to help with that statement, the shop offers more than 120 type styles and 30 standard inks that can be matched to a custom color.

DEMPSEY & CARROLL

Established in 1878

1049 Lexington Avenue
Upper East Side, Manhattan
212-570-4800
www.dempseyandcarroll.com
Subway: 6 train to 77th Street
Open Monday–Wednesday:
10:00 a.m. to 6:00 p.m.
Thursday: 10:00 a.m. to 7:00 p.m.
Friday: 10:00 a.m. to 6:00 p.m.
Saturday: 11:00 a.m. to 6:00 p.m.
Closed Sunday

At the heart of any custom engraved stationery is its motif. Be it a company trademark, a family crest, or any other piece of art, the motif is what really sets personalized stationery apart. The hand-engraving process Dempsey & Carroll uses to create the motif hasn't changed since the 19th century. Engravers start by cutting the relief image of the motif into steel dies and copper plates, similar to the process used to manufacture coins. The plates and dies are then placed into a press, which quickly inks and wipes off the excess before each impression. Cotton-fiber paper is fed into the press by hand as 3,000 pounds of pressure is applied to the paper. Some stationery is given a "bruise," which is an impression on the motif, giving it a tactile, three-dimensional feel. This kind of high-quality personalized stationery is probably not as expensive as you would think. The price per piece is actually not that much more expensive than buying greeting cards off the store rack.

According to Arnold, the real value of personalized stationery is how it really sets you apart from the crowd. "When you're sending a note, it's really like sending a gift to the person you're writing to," he said. "It's a pleasure to open a hand-addressed envelope. People always go for those first. People now have so many choices of communication. Given all those options, it does make the handwritten note that much more special. Handwriting notes is just by definition a different format. You think about what you're saying a little differently. You use complete sentences. You think through your thoughts, the point you're trying to make, the things you want to touch on. You have all of that planned out in your head as you're writing."

One might suspect that the recent communication revolution would be the death knell of stationery. According to Arnold, quite the opposite is true. "I'm a little bit of a stationery freak. I write a lot of notes. I send notes for people's birthdays, notes for thank-yous, notes when I see a friend's book mentioned on television, notes for any reason. There are still people out in the world who do that."

First Flight Music School

Private and Group Lessons
www.firstflightmusic.com

Bass
Drums

Piano
Keyboard

est. 1904

De Robertis

176 PASTICCERIA & CAFFÉ

DE ROBERTIS PASTICCERIA AND CAFFE

Established in 1904

176 First Avenue, East Village, Manhattan
www.derobertiscaffe.com
212-674-7137
Subway: L train to First Avenue
Open Monday: 12:00 p.m. to 11:00 p.m.
Tuesday–Thursday: 9:00 a.m. to 11:00 p.m.
Friday–Saturday: 9:00 a.m. to 12:00 a.m.
Sunday: 9:00 a.m. to 11:00 p.m.

When people think of New York's East Village, artists and hipsters immediately come to mind, but there was a time when much of the neighborhood was a bustling immigrant enclave. Italian restaurants, bakeries, and butcher shops lined the avenues with their Jewish, Russian, and German counterparts. Luckily, a few of these old-fashioned places still survive, giving people a true taste of another era. De Robertis Pasticceria and Caffe, a classic Italian pastry shop on First Avenue, is one of these places.

As one longtime customer puts it, "It gives you that sort of European feeling. Everything is homemade, not mass-produced. It is made by a person, not by a recipe sent from the corporate headquarters." This is just one of the reasons De Robertis has managed to keep customers coming in for more than 100 years.

Paolo De Robertis, who learned his pastry-making skills in Italy, opened the shop in 1904. Newly emigrated from Italy, and determined to make his mark in America, he and his family lived above the shop for decades and everyone pitched in. Paolo's grandson and current co-owner John De Robertis remembers days from his youth working in the store. "My father and mother used to work in the store and when they got a little busy, instead of calling us up on the phone, they used to knock on the steam pipe. We knew when we heard that sound that we needed to go down and help them out." These days, it is still a family affair, with John's sister, Anna; brothers, Paul and Michael; and children, John and Dana, all pitching in.

If Paolo were to come back today, he would be pleasantly surprised at the state of the shop. Other than the addition of a high-definition flat-screen television, not much has changed over the years. De Robertis is luckily one of those places where the owners understand the concept of "If it ain't broke, don't fix it." The recipes the shop uses are the same as when it opened, and much of the decor—from the ornate tiled floor and pressed tin ceiling to the vintage display counters—is original.

Then there's the wonderful backroom dining area, quite likely the only one of its kind in the city. It is an original early 20th-century space, exquisitely decorated in ornate tiles, some of which are hand-painted with delicate motifs. All of it gives the place a classic atmosphere perfectly suited to sitting down and savoring a pastry and coffee. In fact, one gentleman has been coming in for 60 years, ordering the same pastry and coffee every day. This authenticity has not been lost on Hollywood. Scenes from Woody Allen's film *Manhattan Murder Mystery* and Spike Lee's *Malcolm X* were shot here.

All its wonderful decor and friendly atmosphere aside, the shop would not have survived all these years if not for its delicious pastries. The old-world delights are made by hand and from scratch downstairs in a tiny bakery reminiscent of a cramped European kitchen. Some of the baking tools even date back to Paolo's days.

On average, the shop offers a couple hundred items at a time, with bakers working seven days a week. All the classic Italian pastries are here, like crunchy biscotti, anisette toast, and, of course, the Italian hot dog: cannoli. One of its latest additions is cheesecake on a stick—a miniature slice of cheesecake dipped in chocolate and embedded with a stick so customers can eat it like a Popsicle. De Robertis also offers an array of wedding and specialty cakes made to order.

There is one dessert that not only tickles the taste buds, but also may make customers blush. Called a cassatine, it consists of marzipan and cannoli cream filling inside with white icing and a cherry on top. You won't be the first if you think this item looks strangely like a woman's breast. "We used to call them Jane Russells because she was a favorite movie star back in the 1940s and '50s, but now we call them all different names," said De Robertis. "Whoever the famous movie star of the day is, that's what we call them."

Last but not least is the coffee—classic Italian fare made the old-fashioned way, not ruined with trendy syrups or gimmicks. Co-owner Anna Mansueto said she is sometimes amused when Starbucks or Dunkin' Donuts customers come in and tell her she's not making it right. "I've been doing this for the last 48 years of my life," she said. "I know what I'm doing."

Obviously, Mansueto's way is the right way, for a business does not survive for more than 100 years on ambiance alone. Not to mention it is located in a neighborhood that has gone through more cultural transformations than any other place in the city.

"We work very hard to keep a family tradition going here, and I can't believe the love that I have for this store. It's unconditional," said Mansueto. "I just want to see it keep going for many generations to come."

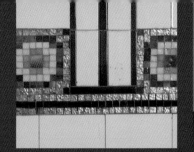

DEVON SHOPS

Established in 1929

111 East 27th Street, Flatiron District, Manhattan
www.devonshop.com 212-686-1760
Subway: 4 or 6 train to 28th Street
Open Monday–Wednesday, Friday: 10:00 a.m. to 6:00 p.m.
Thursday: 10:00 a.m. to 8:00 p.m.
Saturday–Sunday: 12:00 p.m. to 6:00 p.m.

People often walk by the elegant storefront of Devon Shops on East 27th Street thinking it is merely a furniture showroom. Granted, it does sell perhaps some of the finest furniture in Manhattan. But that is only half the story, for unbeknownst to most, every piece of furniture sold by Devon Shops is custom-made on the premises. It is a reminder of when manufacturers and artisans defined New York City.

"I think when people come in, they are pretty surprised that anything like this can be done in America," said owner Charlotte Barbakow. "Even in Europe, most of the small factories have closed, but we are still making wonderful furniture."

Charlotte Barbakow acquired Devon Shops back in 1980 from the Devon family, who had been importing and fabricating furniture since 1929. The name is a bit confusing for some, but it's a nod to the 1940s. Back then, the term "shops" was a catchall phrase for when a business did it all under one roof. In other words, each department—upholstery, finishing, etc.—was its own "shop" even though they were all part of the same business. To this day, that's how Devon Shops works.

In the downstairs workshop, wood comes in as raw lumber and leaves as intricately cut pieces of one-of-a-kind furniture. Craftsmen work with modern and ancient tools—sometimes just a hammer and chisel—to create exquisite carved pieces of furniture. Each employee has a particular specialty, and they often give each other a hand. Barbakow is often down in the workshop, supervising as much as admiring the work of her employees. Everything is made to order, with the customer approving each step of the process. In fact, Barbakow often escorts the customers down to the workshop to see their pieces being made, which is part of the appeal.

Devon Shops specializes in French design—Louis XV and Louis XVI—with a little English and Regency thrown in for good measure. The types of furniture offered include cabinets, dining room tables and chairs, sofas, ottomans, loveseats, armoires, and beds. Armoires are the shop's specialty; they can be customized for entertainment systems, bars, or miniature work stations.

In addition to being custom-made, pieces from Devon Shops are exceptional in both quality and materials. "There is a big difference between hand-carved furniture and pressed furniture," said Barbakow. "You can run your hand over it and feel how sharp it is; it's like cut glass. Once you are in the showroom, the quality speaks for itself." Hand-tied coilsprings, horse hair, and goose down are all part of the shop's refined construction. Its hand-rubbed wood finishes—including all 30 variations of hand-wiped painted finishes available—are considered some of the best in the country.

And despite its elegant and delicate look, the furniture is made to last, to be passed down to the next generation. "Nobody acquires our furniture to put it in the living room and use it as a museum. This furniture is meant to be used," said Barbakow. And while it can be pricey—as is the case for anything custom-made—you can be sure you are getting a unique piece. "It's a personal thing, like when you buy art. You don't want your apartment to look like anyone else's," she said.

EAR INN

Established in 1817

326 Spring Street, SoHo, Manhattan
212-431-9750 www.earinn.com
Subway: A, C, or E train to Spring Street
Open daily 12:00 p.m. to 4:00 a.m.

On the western end of Spring Street in SoHo, one would be hard-pressed to find anything that would indicate this was once part of the epicenter of America's seafaring trade. But at one time, long forgotten docks along the Hudson River were loaded with longshoremen and ships sending and receiving goods from around the world. They are all gone now, the docks pretty much replaced by the West Side Highway and the warehouses replaced by luxury condos. But luckily, one remnant of that colorful past survives. It's a remarkably well-preserved mariner's bar: the Ear Inn.

The Ear Inn is first and foremost a neighborhood bar, but it is also a piece of living history, a snapshot of New York City's past. Customers can feel it the moment they walk into the place—from the creaking floorboards to the artifacts dating all the way back to the 17th century lining the walls and shelves. The building itself is one of the last of its kind in the city, a three-story brick and wood beamed Federal-style structure built in 1817. When it was built, the Hudson River was just five feet from its doorstep. Progress and land-fill have pushed the shoreline to its present location a block away. Time has even shrunk the building. It is now a few feet lower thanks to its foundation slowly sinking into the ground.

Just like any building that's been around for that long, it has quite a few tales to tell. The building was first owned by a freed slave named James Brown, who at one time was an aide to George Washington. Some historians believe the iconic painting of Washington crossing the Delaware River depicts Brown as one of the rowers. Brown owned the building for several years, living upstairs and running a tobacco shop on the first floor.

After Brown passed away, the building went through several incarnations, including a boarding house and eventually brewery and bar run by Thomas Cloak. Not surprisingly, it soon became a haven for sailors and waterfront workers, getting quite a rough-and-tumble reputation in the process. For years, it was rumored to be a brothel and smugglers' den. In fact, to this day there are several small bedrooms upstairs with locks on all the doors.

During much of the 20th century, the place was known as a "morning bar," open each day only until noon. Union dockworkers would punch in at the local union hall and wait at the bar for work. If there was no work, many were paid anyway just for showing up for the allotted time, a process known as being "union featherbedded." For years, quite a collection of crusty old dockcrawlers drank their mornings away at the bar, barring women and strangers from entering the place.

By the early 1970s, the bar had been run into the ground. It was given new life when Rip Hayman, then a student at New York University, came into the picture. He spent some 30 years renovating the place, eventually buying it along with business partner Martin Sheridan. "I got in because I told the bartender I'd fix the roof if he'd let me live upstairs," said Hayman. He thinks part of the reason the building is still standing is because of the quality of the wood they found used in the structural beams and floorboards. "This is old-growth spruce, so the wood was harvested in the late 1700s. The wood itself may be up to 400 years old. It has about four times the structural strength of any current wood."

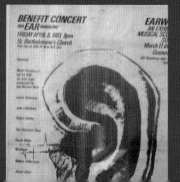

As Hayman and his friends began to restore the place, they found fascinating slices of its former lives. In the basement, a cornucopia of artifacts were sprung from under the floor—many of them from the Colonial era. Old pipes, plates, and animal bones with butcher marks all tell the story of a tavern ripe with activity. They even found evidence of the Great Fire of 1776 that burned a major part of New York City. Hand-hewn base beams complete with ax marks still show scorch marks from that time. And when they discovered pieces of original wooden Colonial-era sidewalks, they promptly refitted them outside the bar. But not all the finds are from Colonial times. Hayman discovered in the chimney a revolver dating back to the 1920s, which was probably ditched after a crime. As Hayman said, "You don't throw a good gun away just because you don't like the look of it."

For many years, the bar did not even have a proper name. For a time it was known as the Green Door, named unceremoniously after, you guessed it, its front door. Then Hayman and his pals christened it the Ear Inn. "The neon sign used to say 'BAR.' And then we were publishing a music magazine here called *Ear Magazine*. So, we went out there and painted the ends of the 'B' with black paint so 'B' became 'E.' That was partly because the landmark's commission wouldn't allow any new sign. So it became the Ear Inn. The old-timers never noticed; they all thought it was just busted."

A couple of years ago, the Ear Inn got a lucky break— new next-door neighbors. Most of the time, preservationists are wary when modern buildings go up in historical neighborhoods, but this time it was a blessing. The new neighbor was the Urban Glass House, famed architect Phillip Johnson's last creation. As part of the land deal, financiers for the project agreed to help shore up the Ear Inn's structural integrity, put on a new roof, and renovate the basement—all maintenance that was desperately needed.

As this little Federal building in the out-of-the-way place continues to entertain and fascinate, its caretakers are making sure to share and carry on its eclectic legacy by hosting art openings and music events regularly. In fact, the Ear Inn's poetry series is the second oldest in the city. Some of its events attracted the likes of John Lennon, Tom Waits, and Allen Ginsberg.

Today, the Ear Inn attracts all kinds of New Yorkers from different backgrounds who come for a taste of history, not to mention a great menu that serves an eclectic variety of dishes, including grilled salmon, cowboy chili, and sirloin or turkey burgers. The owners also open the place up to children, giving school groups tours of living history.

As the decades roll by, the Ear Inn's purpose in the city becomes more evident. "It's not the glitz and the glamour; it's the warmth and the camaraderie and the friendship," said one longtime customer. "You can get a great glass of beer here and a great meal. And you'll meet interesting characters from all walks of life."

ECONOMY CANDY

Established in 1937

108 Rivington Street, Lower East Side, Manhattan
212-254-1531 www.economycandy.com
Subway: J, M, or Z to Essex Street
Open Sunday–Friday: 9:00 a.m. to 6:00 p.m.
Saturday: 10:00 a.m. to 5:00 p.m.

Everyone has a favorite candy from their childhood, and perhaps even a favorite candy store. For many New Yorkers, that candy store still exists. Located on Rivington Street, Economy Candy is one of the last classic retail shops left on the Lower East Side. Once filled with pushcarts and immigrant merchants, today trendy bistros and boutiques rule the neighborhood.

But Economy Candy, still buzzing with activity reminiscent of those old shops of yore, does just fine with its new neighbors. Inside is a medium-sized retail space filled with every sugar-infused concoction one could imagine. The thousands upon thousands of brightly colored wrappers and boxes on display are a visual treat. Shelves, some more than nine feet high, line the walls, stuffed with candy from every corner of the world. Lining the ceiling are shelves filled with antique candy dispensers, boxes, and advertisements from the owner's personal collection.

Going into its third generation of ownership, Economy Candy is run by the Cohen Family. "My father's brother-in-law's father started this store in 1937 as a shoe store and converted it to a candy store after the war," said owner Jerry Cohen. "When my father got out of the Army with his brother-in-law, they came into the business and started Economy Candy."

From high-end chocolates to Pop Rocks, there is something for everyone at Economy Candy. Have a favorite candy from your youth? The store most certainly will have it. But the store doesn't sell just *any* sweets. Cohen has a rigorous testing program. "It's got to be tested and Jerry-approved. I

buy what I like," he said. "I eat all day long. I mean, I love candy. I don't weigh 98 pounds."

It is not just nostalgia and variety that brings people to Economy Candy, though. Regulars know that this place is a genuine New York bargain. Cohen buys direct from the manufacturers, so prices are often close to wholesale—one of the reasons their online business receives orders from around the country. Plus, the customer service is top-notch. "If a customer is thinking of a candy bar they had when they were growing up, I'll know what it is," said Cohen.

Weekends at Economy Candy prove that Cohen must be doing something right. The store is jam-packed with children and adults overstimulated by the sweet sights and smells even before any sugar has had a chance to touch their tongues. Helping out on these busy days are about a dozen high schoolers. The Cohens believe in hiring only local kids so they can give back to a neighborhood that has been so good to them. The kids get a little pocket change and learn important business skills, which at least one former employee has used to start his own business—a health food shop—just a few doors down. The Cohen family's goodwill stretches across the world, too; Economy Candy regularly sends free sweets to third-world countries like Sudan.

"It's a happy business. What we have is a good, solid business," said Cohen. "Candy is happiness. You leave your calories at the door; you leave your judgment at the door. You just come in and be a kid again. You run around the store, you take a basket, you fill it up, and hopefully that $5 goes a long way."

10 lb Bag Candy $18.00

ECONOMY CANDY

108 RIVINGTON ST

ECONOMY CANDY
108 ECONOMY CANDY
Tel: 254-1531
economycandy.com

OLD TIME FAVORITES 75¢ each

EISENBERG'S SANDWICH SHOP

Established in 1929

174 Fifth Avenue, Flatiron District, Manhattan
www.eisenbergsnyc.com 212-675-5096
Subway: N or R train to 23rd Street
Open Monday–Friday: 6:30 a.m. to 8:00 p.m.
Saturday: 9:00 a.m. to 6:00 p.m.
Sunday: 9:00 a.m. to 5:00 p.m.

There is something to be said about a sandwich shop that has been able to survive in Manhattan for more than 80 years. It is an especially grand feat in the ultratrendy Flatiron District, where everything can be oh-so-last-week. Across the street from the historic Flatiron Builiding, Eisenberg's Sandwich Shop has stood the test of time by offering people two things: good food and good company.

Carl Eisenberg opened the sandwich shop in 1929, and his family ran it until the 1960s. After being a customer for 15 years, Josh Konecky took over the business in 2006. "I always wanted to get into the food business," he said. "Having been a customer here, I always liked Eisenberg's, so I bought it. I really do feel like right now it's my turn to look after this. When I first took the store over, customers said, 'Oh, you're gonna change it.' I said, 'No, I'm really not. I'm just gonna clean it up a little.'"

The shop is pretty simple. It is one of those classic lunch counters straight out of an Edward Hopper painting or film noir movie. Its decor is not lost on its customers, who appreciate the 1930s-era original fixtures, such as dark wood paneling, steel diner stools, and even gas-fired coffeemakers.

All of the decor lends itself well to the community feel of the place, sometimes a rarity in New York City. "It's like a community," said waiter Robert Friedman. "People come here. We know their names and they know us. It's special." Although the bulk of its business is regulars, it is also somewhere strangers feel comfortable enough to strike up conversations with one another.

Businesses can't survive in New York City on quaintness alone, though. The food must be spectacular. But that's no problem for Eisenberg's. "This place is about two things: matzo ball soup and chocolate egg creams," said one loyal customer. "That's what I always get and I've been coming here for 30 years. It's for the food. That's what Eisenberg's is all about."

Its menu is simple, but done right. It is *the* place to buy sandwiches, and all the classics are here—ham and cheese, tuna fish, and egg salad. The shop even cooks its own roast beef and turkey in-house. When Konecky took over, he added a few dinner entrees—like hamburgers and fried clams—but kept the rest of the menu the same. It also has a full breakfast menu.

Unlike delis with premade sandwiches, Eisenberg's makes everything to order. "People will come in, especially younger people, and say, 'So what comes on the chicken salad sandwich?'" said Konecky. "I say, 'Whatever you want to put on the chicken salad sandwich. I'll put chocolate syrup on it. I don't care.'"

After chowing down on one of the great sandwiches, customers can polish their meal off with something from the vintage soda fountain, like egg creams, milk shakes, or even lime rickeys. Eisenberg's even brews its own iced tea.

In a neighborhood known for its astronomical rent prices, many regulars worry how long Eisenberg's has left here. Luckily, according to Konecky, the shop still has several years left on its lease. He makes a point of thanking customers for continuing to come in, for it is those regulars that keep the institution alive. "There's so little of old New York still around," he said. "I feel like I'm doing my part to keep it alive."

In the year of 1879, Albert Einstein was born, the incandescent light bulb was introduced to the public, and in Lower Manhattan E. Vogel Custom Boots and Shoes first opened for business. After all these years it is still at it, handcrafting one-of-a-kind boots and shoes, specially made for each customer. It is now also one of the last makers of handcrafted, custom-made goods of any kind left in Manhattan. All of its work is done in-house by a dozen master cobblers who are helping to carry on one family's legacy through three centuries.

The company was established by German immigrant Egidius Vogel. Now, his great-grandsons, Jack Lynch and Dean Vogel, and Vogel's father, Hank, run the company, making some of the finest footwear in the world. There are several reasons why one would spend the money on a custom-made pair of shoes. "It's really a superior fit to anything you're going to buy off-the-rack because very few people have the exact same right and left foot," said Lynch. "The other advantage to getting custom footwear is you can get what you want. In a way, it's like ordering a car. There are several options on everything we do and the customer is literally designing it, whether it is a boot or a shoe, from the bottom up."

Walking through the five stories of E. Vogel's small brick factory is like stepping back in time. The rich smell of leather permeates the air. Cobbler tools line the walls; many look like they belong in an antique shop, but show evidence of daily use. There are bits and pieces of leather and other shoe ingredients all over the place. E. Vogel looks all over the world to find the best material for footwear, but much of the leather comes from France. Not only are the French known to have some of the best calf tanners in the world, the calves in the region are also somewhat smaller than their American counterparts, giving them a softer, more supple skin with a very tight grain.

Creating a pair of E. Vogel shoes takes about a week's worth of work. The first step is to take circumference measurements of the customer's feet. From that, a shoe "last" is created, which is a wood model of each foot. Next, a paper pattern is made of the shoe's design, using the last as a guide. From there, the leather pieces are taken to the upper-making department to be cut from the pattern and sewed together. Finally, the leather is stretched over the last by hand. "Very few companies make shoes this way," said Lynch. "There is no machine that can get this leather to sit onto this last the way these guys can do it with water and a hammer. That creates superior fit. It also produces a shoe that wears and breaks the way it's supposed to in the right places."

In the finishing department, the shoe is given a sole. If it is a boot, it is then fully soaked and wooden blocks are hammered into the shaft of the boot, giving it its shape. The final step is a polish and heal balance. "When the customer puts his foot in the shoe and steps on the ground, it feels beautiful," said Lynch.

E. Vogel is best known for its equestrian riding boots. Everyone from Charles Lindbergh to Jacqueline Kennedy Onassis has had their feet fitted for a pair. E. Vogel has fulfilled large orders for boots to outfit cadets at Texas A&M University and the U.S. Olympic equestrian team, but it also caters to the individual. "I had just brought my new Vogel golf shoes to the course and someone noticed they looked like they had never been worn before," said one recent customer. "He said, 'You can't use a brand-new pair of golf shoes without breaking them in.' I told him, 'You can if they were custom-made for you.' They feel even better than a well-worn store-bought pair of shoes."

E. Vogel shoes are not cheap. Prices start around $1,375, but with each subsequent pair a customer buys, the price goes down several hundred dollars. It is money well spent when you consider that a well-worn pair can last more than 20 years.

E. VOGEL CUSTOM BOOTS AND SHOES

Established in 1879

19 Howard Street
SoHo, Manhattan
www.vogelboots.com
212-925-2460
Subway: N, R, or 6 train
to Canal Street
Open Monday–Friday:
8:00 a.m. to 4:30 p.m.
Saturday:
8:00 a.m. to 2:00 p.m.

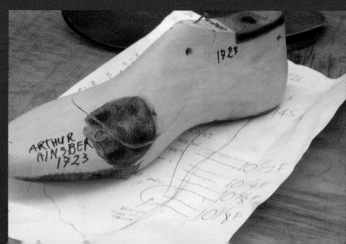

You might think that fountain pens have gone the way of cuff links and record vinyl—something to wax nostalgia about from the "good old days." Step into the Fountain Pen Hospital on Warren Street and you will be happily surprised. This shop buzzes with activity, with salesmen eagerly waiting on shoppers of all walks of life—bankers, politicians, students, and tourists—each looking to step up their penmanship.

The Fountain Pen Hospital's showroom boasts the largest selection of pens in the world, with some 4,000 on display. High-quality ballpoints, roller balls, and the shop's signature item—finely made fountain pens—can range in price from $5 to an astonishing $65,000. "You would think this kind of business would be dying, but we are very unique in what we do and customer service is very, very important to us so we just keep building and building," said co-owner Terry Wiederlight.

The business began in 1946, when fountain pens were as common as fedoras. Wiederlight's father, Phillip, and grandfather, Albert, both had a knack for mechanical things and started tinkering with pens. Later, they opened a repair service in downtown Manhattan. Today, pen repair is largely overshadowed by the shop's retail side, but the "hospital" moniker has stuck. Part of the store's success is knowing when to change with the times. In the late 1970s, when fountain pens fell out of favor due to the invasion of cheap ballpoint pens, the store switched over to selling office supplies in order to stay afloat. In the 1980s, big chain stores like Staples came in and took away *that* business, so the Fountain Pen Hospital went back to its roots. Luckily, fountain pens were coming back into style.

Today, Terry Wiederlight runs the business with his brother, Steve, and some 15 employees. A robust website and quarterly catalog helps the company boast more than 75,000 customers worldwide.

Through the years the business has served its share of well-known personalities, including Ernest Hemingway, Betty Grable, and Count Basie. More recent customers include Tom Hanks, General Colin Powell, and Arnold Schwarzenegger. But one celebrity customer stands out, not for his fame but for his friendship: Bill Cosby. "We have been friends for 15 years, and he has been such an unbelievable person for us," said Wiederlight. "He has even gone to the point of mentioning us on *Late Show with David Letterman* and *Live with Regis and Kathie Lee*."

And it's understandable why Cosby and countless others love the Fountain Pen Hospital's finely made pens. First, there is the quality penmanship they allow, for the ink flows better and easier, thus giving a better script. Also, the pen's nib is more sensitive and responsive to the person's touch and actually gives a better portrayal of one's unique penmanship. Thus, the user's personality and emotion come out more when using a fountain pen.

A finely made pen is more than a writing instrument. With the countless varieties and designs available, there are pens for every walk of life and taste. There are pens made of every imaginable material—copper, steel, leather, gold, diamonds, and even cooled lava, mammoth ivory, and bamboo. Styles are also across the board—from vintage celluloid pens as colorful as the day they were made to modern pens with abstract shapes and designs. Themes can be classic to quirky—from limited-edition Beatles pens to pens shaped like crayons. There are even pens infused with authentic historical artifacts. Take for instance the Krone brand Abraham Lincoln pen, which has actual DNA from the president himself fused into the pen cap.

Keeping up with the times, the Fountain Pen Hospital now sells pens with an iPad stylus embedded on the other end. Still, bells and whistles aside, there's something simple and wonderful about a finely made fountain pen. "Pull out a beautiful pen and it can really start a conversation," said Wiederlight. "It can also help mark a special occasion. I mean, when you go to a real estate closing or contract signing, the lawyer's not going to pull out a Bic," he said, smiling.

FOUNTAIN PEN HOSPITAL

Established in 1946

10 Warren Street
City Hall, Manhattan
www.fountainpenhospital.com
212-964-0580
Subway: 2 or 3 train to Park Place;
A or C train to Chambers Street;
R or W train to City Hall
Open Monday–Friday:
7:45 a.m. to 5:30 p.m.

GLASER'S BAKE SHOP

Established in 1902

1670 First Avenue, Yorkville, Manhattan
www.glasersbakeshop.com 212-289-2562
Subway: 4, 5, or 6 train to 86th Street
Open Tuesday–Friday: 7:00 a.m. to 7:00 p.m.
Saturday: 8:00 a.m. to 7:00 p.m.
Sunday: 8:00 a.m. to 3:00 p.m.
Closed Monday

For some businesses, part of the appeal is the fact that they serve as a living link to the past. They allow a neighborhood to hold onto its history and past regardless of the inevitable changes. Residents of Yorkville have this type of business in Glaser's Bake Shop. This German American bakery has stayed wondrously the same as its surroundings transformed from a thriving immigrant neighborhood to a gentrified bedroom community. The Glaser family, now in its third generation of ownership, has been baking at the same location since 1902.

Daily offerings include German delicacies like Bavarian cookies, Springerle, and bundt cake, as well as doughnuts, cookies, tea biscuits, and even the occasional trendy cupcake. The apple strudel is often made with fruit from the family's own orchard in upstate New York. German baked goods reign supreme, but as co-owner Herb Glaser put it, "We're pretty well Americanized, so whatever sells we try to make. The all-American brownie is our best seller." Like more traditional bakeries, there are different goods offered each day. The shop even posts its daily offerings on Facebook for customers.

German immigrants John and Justine Glaser first opened a bakery near Bloomingdale's in Midtown. While visiting Yorkville to attend nearby Saint Joseph's Church, the Glasers surmised that the neighborhood could use their baking services. (At the time, East 86th Street was often referred to as "German Broadway.") Soon afterward, they bought a building and opened up Glaser's Bake Shop. And in true mom-and-pop fashion, they even moved upstairs.

Today, not much has changed. Glaser descendants still live and work here. John and Justine's grandchildren—brothers

Herb and John—do most of the baking by themselves. Upon entering the bakery, one will almost always see one of the brothers baking away. Incredibly, they work on the original wooden baker's table and with many of the same baking tools that their grandfather used. The brothers still close the shop during July and part of August, partly to keep their grandfather's tradition from the old country alive, and partly because the shop doesn't have air conditioning.

As for the bakery's interior, it is an amazing piece of New York City history in itself. Most of the fixtures date back to 1918, giving the place the warmth and feeling of that era. Large dark oak cabinets line the shop, showing off cakes and family mementos. John Glaser's original recipe book—which is filled with recipes written in German—is among these mementos. The brothers still use it today.

The great baked goods and historic decor aside, it is the shop's authenticity and tradition that make its customers so loyal. "Christmastime brings people back to the old neighborhood, all the way from Jersey, Queens, or Long Island, to get their traditional Stollen (fruit cake) and German cookies because they can't get them anywhere else," said employee Rita Callahan. Plus, Glaser's is a daily ritual for some. It is place where many people come to just hang out and shoot the breeze. One such patron is Willy, an elderly German American who parks himself by the counter and occasionally pitches in with sweeping and helping with orders. "It reminds me of a German home. People are nice; they come and talk," he said. His words do a good job of summing up Glaser's Bake Shop—it is not just a place to get a sugar fix, but a place to call home.

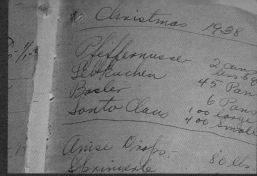

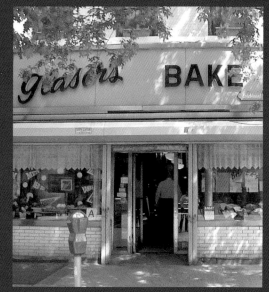

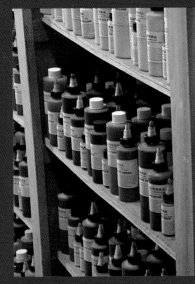

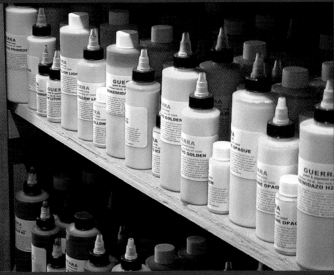

GUERRA PAINT AND PIGMENT

Established in 1986

510 East 13th Street
East Village, Manhattan
www.guerrapaint.com
212-529-0628
Subway: L train to First Avenue
Open Monday–Saturday:
12:00 p.m. to 7:00 p.m.

Sometimes a person is compelled to start a business due to his or her own needs as a consumer. Guerra Paint and Pigment is one of those places, created because one man thought there must be a better way. Founder and co-owner Art Guerra got the idea to start his own pigment supply shop in the 1970s when he could not find quality paints. "I got hired by CIDA, which was Jimmy Carter giving artists in New York City jobs. I was the first government-hired artist to do murals since the WPA back in the 1930s. So I went out and bought these paints for signs. They wouldn't mix well and were all-around poor quality," said Guerra.

Instead of using these inferior paints, Guerra began making his own paints, becoming a pigment connoisseur for the art field and opening up a shop in the East Village in 1986. "Artists were always discovering me because East 13th Street was one of the biggest drug blocks in New York at that time. They would come down here to get their drugs and see my little store. They were always so floored to see how quick and easy it is to make your own paint," he said. Now, along with co-owners Jody Bretnall and Seren Morey, Guerra supplies the art world with pigments—not only in New York City, but worldwide.

To most, Guerra Paint and Pigment just looks like a paint store. And it is, but to be more specific, it is a pigment supplier. Whether it's for vinyl, acrylic, watercolor, or any other paints, customers can work with more than 200 powdered or liquid pigment concentrates to create their own paint. The pigment can also be used as a tinting agent for other materials, like grout, stucco, or cement. Guerra also offers metallic, pearlescent, or glitter additives—along with fillers like pumice and ultra-fine glass beads—to give the paint a unique texture.

Why go to all the trouble of making your own paint? First, it is just plain fun. But for more pragmatic reasons, it is about quality and control. The dirty little secret in the paint world is that over-the-counter paint is not all that great. Core ingredients like raw pigment and resin are expensive, so it is no surprise that manufacturers skimp as much as possible, which leaves customers with a paint that fades fast and is hard to control. Need proof? Notice how many outdoor signs that are 20 years old look just as faded as ones painted before World War II. "At our store, you can use as much pigment as you want, making it much more vibrant than a premade paint," said Bretnall. "Also, if you put it down big and thick, it's going to stay that way. It's not going to collapse and shrink."

Guerra Paint and Pigment does not actually make the raw pigments itself. It is more like a depository for pigments and pigment conservationists. The world of pigment manufacturing is a complicated one. Pure pigments are not just "dialed up" on a computer using something like Photoshop. Most are created for a specific application by a specific company. Pigments are being discovered and becoming extinct all the time due to demand and cost-effectiveness. "See this cream color?" said Bretnall, pointing to a sample. "It is the actual pigment Buick used on its cream-colored cars in the 1950s and '60s. We have the last 200 pounds of it."

Many pure pigments are first developed by companies for the auto industry due to its need for high quality and durability. "Artists get the hand-me-downs of what's available in the industrial market," said co-owner Seren Morey. This means the owners at Guerra are on a perpetual treasure hunt, going to the ends of the earth for pigments.

Sometimes it is a case of one man's trash is another man's treasure. Some companies are glad to get rid of their discontinued pigments, selling them for pennies on the dollar. "A lot of these pigments would end up covered with spiderwebs and sitting in these dark corners," said Guerra. "I would phone the company up and they'd say, 'Sure, we have a whole corner full of old stuff that we don't want.'" Like Blue 80, which Guerra acquired from a plant in Germany. The pigment was to be used on a high-end Porsche automobile but did not make the final cut. And Crap Green, which is literally the residue a certain pigment company ends up with after it cleans its pigment manufacturing tanks. "It's ugly as hell," said Bretnall, "but very popular with artists."

The small one-room shop is very popular, and just as colorful as one might imagine. Upon entering, customers are immediately greeted by an enormous color chart that takes up most of the shop's left wall. The chart shows pigment offerings in various textures, opacities, and sheens so that customers can see the limitless possibilities right away. The second half of the shop, stuffed with shelf after shelf of bottles and vials of liquid and powdered pigments, looks like some kind of hyperchromatic pharmacy or mad scientist's laboratory.

Once a customer picks a pigment, the owners are almost insistent on giving first-time users a quick lesson on how to use the pigments with different types of bases and binders for different effects. The initial application is a rewarding one, for it is quite amazing how little pigment is needed to create a vibrant burst of color. Also, with just a few stirs, the colors seem fresher and livelier than paint out of a can.

Artists, designers, average Joes—just about anyone looking for color comes to Guerra Paint and Pigment. And the shop's products have been used on countless items, including stage sets for the Metropolitan Opera and Cirque du Soleil and Lady Gaga's concert tour piano. Oprah Winfrey's house in Hawaii even has some Guerra pigment in it. "One of the things that we've always prided ourselves on is that we're totally artist-run," said Art Guerra. "Anybody that works here is a painter and loves working with this material." It's a good thing, too, for New York City is always craving a little more color.

GUERRA
paint & pigment corp.
310 East 13th St. New York, NY 10009
HOLOGRAPHIC JEWELS

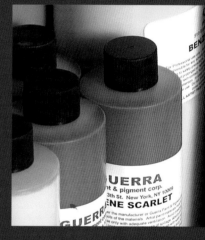

Holographic Studios—a hologram manufacturer that also has a small in-house gallery—is the oldest of its kind in the world and is going into its fourth decade of business. Located on a quiet residential street in the neighborhood of Kips Bay, it is hardly the place one would expect to find cutting-edge technology. "Very often people think that we just opened and they wish us luck," said owner and hologram pioneer Jason Sapan. "Then we tell them we've been here for more than 30 years and they're all shocked."

Inside, Holographic Studios is an interesting mix of old and new, historic and experimental. The cluttered gallery is full of hundreds of examples of holograms uniquely displayed along the brick walls. The building itself is a classic brick brownstone, which was originally a blacksmith's shop about 150 years ago.

Sapan dreamed up the studio when the science of holography was still in its infancy. Now, his place is New York City's only commercial holographic laboratory and gallery. The studio's bread-and-butter is making custom holograms for commercial clients, which include the science and entertainment industries. The studio does a wide variety of projects: advertising premiums, museum pieces, anti-piracy detection, cover art for CDs, and family portraits.

Over the years, an eclectic group of people has visited the studio, including former New York City mayor Ed Koch and musician Billy Idol, who—according to Sapan—was particularly interested in the technology and process. Sapan has also created hologram portraits of comedians Phyllis Diller and The Smothers Brothers, talk show host Phil Donohue, and former president Bill Clinton, who was the first living president to sit for a hologram portrait.

Sapan has even made hologram art out of artists themselves, like pop icon Andy Warhol. He said Warhol was very easy to work with. "Usually it takes hours to get people to do exactly what you want, but with his white shock of hair and his really strong cheekbones, the dimension was just there and I had just the right combination of hard and soft lighting

to make him look very, very strong and Warholesque, for lack of a better word," he said.

Sapan's expertise in holograms and lasers has also been used in movies like Tom Cruise's *Vanilla Sky* and at the infamous Studio 54 nightclub. One of his projects even netted him a starring role in one of the first music videos: "(It's Not Me) Talking" by Flock of Seagulls. The band asked if Sapan could do lasers shooting out of a spaceship, and he assured them that he could. During the process of creating laser effects for the video, the director asked Sapan if he would like to be in it. He agreed, and became the radar guy.

Many people are unfamiliar with holograms, but making one is less complex than one would think. It is similar to creating a conventional photograph. Basically, a hologram is a photograph of light waves. When light hits an object, it takes its shape and then bounces back onto film, which is developed into a photograph of those shaped light waves. To photograph something as a hologram, an object is set up and lit, and then laser beams are aimed at a series of mirrors and optics. The object is placed in a completely dark room, which essentially acts as the body of the camera. Light waves reflected from the object are recorded on holographic film. The film is then developed using nearly the same process as conventional photographs, the main difference being that photos developed in the holographic studio will not reveal an image, but rather will reveal the pattern of light waves.

According to Sapan, the detail that can be achieved in holograms is astonishing. "Let's say we have a hologram of a woman's face and there is a drop of water on her face," he said. "We could take a microscope to that drop of water on her face and focus down, and if there was an amoeba floating in the water we could focus down and look at the nucleus and the mitochondria of that amoeba, all in the hologram. It's an incredibly powerful technology and its applications have only begun to be imagined."

HOLOGRAPHIC STUDIOS

Established in 1979

240 East 26th Street
Kips Bay, Manhattan
www.holographer.com
www.facebook.com/Holographer
212-686-9397
Subway: 4 or 6 train to 23rd Street
Open Monday–Friday:
12:00 p.m. to 6:00 p.m.
Call to make an appointment.

THE JANE HOTEL

Established in 1908

113 Jane Street
West Village, Manhattan
www.thejanenyc.com
212-924-6700
Subway: A, C, or E train to 14th Street
Open 24 hours a day

A hotel room in New York City for less than $100? Surely, there must be a catch. Maybe dirty rooms with unrecognizable carpet stains? Quite the contrary, for the building has been completely restored top-to-bottom, making it one of the newest hotels in the city.

So what is the catch? Rooms at The Jane Hotel—a boutique luxury hotel overlooking the Hudson River in the most westerly part of the West Village—are inexpensive because of their size: 50 square feet. No, that's not a typo. Average rooms are seven foot by seven foot. Beds are twin size, and for couples, there are bunk beds for $125 a night. The unisex bathrooms are in the hallways. Captain's Cabins are closer to the size of an average hotel room and include their own bathroom. Still, even they are cheaper than the average New York City hotel room.

Bringing new meaning to the term "boutique hotel," The Jane Hotel is " . . . basically a new brand of hotels in America, which is micro hotels. This kind of setup is very familiar to the European set and students around the world," said front office manager A. J. Heekin. Indeed, there have been times some guests are a little taken aback by the size of the rooms. "If someone is used to a chain hotel in the Midwest, which has larger rooms, they might be surprised," said Heekin. "But The Jane is the perfect place in New York because you shouldn't be staying in, you should be up and about."

But even Americans fed on a diet of super-sized everything are delightfully surprised at the manageability and fun of staying in a hotel room this size. Rooms are smartly designed, taking advantage of literally every inch. Storage units fit snuggly under beds, providing necessary dresser space. Fans and televisions are mounted on the wall. Inspired by luxury train cabins from the Pullman car era, the rooms are decorated with stained wood and rich fabric and colors—comparable to any five-star luxury hotel. Like its contemporaries, The Jane Hotel equips its rooms with iPod docks, wi-fi, and full room service. There are even free bicycle rentals. And for that trip down the hall to the bathroom, there are robes and slippers for each guest.

Believe it or not, the rooms at The Jane have always been this size. The building was built in 1908 by the American Seaman's Friend Society for sailors that were used to such close quarters. Architect William A. Boring chose a Georgian-style design for the building, complete with sea motifs like fish and anchors embedded in the brick and stone facade. (Boring is also known for his work on Ellis Island; he designed its immigrant station houses.) Rooms cost 25 cents a night. The society's mission was to give sailors a more "civilized" stay in New York City than lower Manhattan was notoriously known for. Rules, including no alcohol, were strictly enforced. There was also a hefty amount of Christian prophesying on virtue.

In 1912, the hotel was part of international news. It was here that survivors of the *Titanic* were housed after being rescued by the ship *Carpathia*. In fact, Pier 54—where the ship docked just steps from the hotel—still survives. Its cast-iron archway even shows faintly visible paint advertising the White Star and Cunard lines. Many of the rescued sailors ended up staying at the hotel for an extended time while an investigation was conducted into the sinking. Also, because the White Star Line stopped paying the sailors after the sinking, many of them were out of money and out of luck. New Yorkers often stopped by to offer them food, clothes, and money. A plaque in the hotel's lobby commemorates that time. Unfortunately, due to its position on the floor, the plaque has been worn smooth, making it completely unreadable.

In 1944, the building was sold to the YMCA; then, in 1951, it was converted into The Jane West Hotel. After a steady and very thorough decline, which included the installation of bulletproof plexiglass at the reception desk, the hotel was again renamed, this time the Riverview Hotel. Long-term residents paid just $200 a month to live there. It essentially became a flophouse of last resort for countless indigents, drug addicts, and starving artists, including drag queen extraordinaire RuPaul. (Though in those years there was some appreciation for its history; the building was landmarked in 2001.) Residents like RuPaul helped stop the hotel from becoming just a destructive place. "There were great artistic things that happened here even when it was in disrepair. There were live shows in the Jane Street Theater (now the ballroom). In fact, this is where *Hedwig and The Angry Inch* was originally performed," said Heekin.

In 2008, hoteliers Eric Goode and Sean MacPherson—well-known for the Maritime Hotel and the Bowery Hotel—came in and did a complete rehabilitation of the old place. The lobby now has a nouveau-bohemian feel, minus the dirt and grime. Keeping with that classic yet eclectic tone, the bellhops dress in crisp uniforms complete with pillbox hats. Stuffed peacocks and carved wooden moose heads add to the eclectic tone. "I've had people come in and say it reminds them of The Orient Express," said Heekin. Next to the lobby is Cafe Gitane, a dining spot that specializes in French-Moroccan food like spicy meatballs in turmeric tomato sauce and salmon potpie.

Inside the ballroom and bar are a myriad of whimsical visual delights, like stuffed monkeys dressed as bellhops and colorful modern paintings with an abstract twist. Also in the ballroom is one of the most intriguing historical artifacts in all of New York City. It is a gigantic disco ball, looking a little worse for the wear—missing many of its mirror pieces and not without a ding or two on its rusty steel core. But, oh, if this ball could talk—for it is rumored to be from the legendary and decadent nightclub Studio 54. One of the owners bought it for his personal collection and installed it in the hotel.

And what about the tenants who were there before the hotel's miraculous transformation? Don't worry; they too have a happy ending. "It's important to us that we keep the face of this neighborhood, so we have tenants who've stayed with us for years still living here," said Heekin. "Seeing them mix and mingle with our guests is wonderful. It's a reminder of what New York is all about."

No one knows the art of hats better than J. J. Hat Center, which has been selling the headwear in Midtown Manhattan for more than 100 years. It is not only the oldest and largest hat store in New York City but also one of the very last of its kind. Opened in 1911, the store has changed ownership just a few times and has been at its current location on Fifth Avenue near 32nd Street for 20 years.

The shop space has some previous history of its own. It was the first New York City showroom for IBM in the 1920s and still has many of the original fixtures from that era, including ornate reliefs depicting the IBM logo on the walls. Although it now sells hats instead of commercial scales and punch card tabulators, the shop still has an old New York feel to it. Vintage wooden cabinets filled with dozens of hat styles line the two-story space. At any given time, there are nearly 10,000 hats in stock. Don't go looking for baseball or stocking caps here, though. J.J. Hat Center only sells classic, finely made hats, many from the Borsalino Hat Company in Italy, which is well-known for its high-end fedoras made from Belgian rabbit fur.

J. J. Hat Center has customers from all over the world and all walks of life. It even serves celebrity clients—such as actor Pierce Brosnan and rapper Run-DMC—many of whom leave autographed hats for the shop to display. And when you're ready to purchase a quality hat, the knowledgeable employees at J. J. Hat Center will be ready to serve you.

So what styles are the most popular these days? According to general manager Marc Williamson, driving caps, newsboy caps, porkpie hats, and stingy brims are the strongest sellers. In addition, the Indiana Jones style of hat, popularized by Harrison Ford in *Raiders of the Lost Ark*, continues to be a top seller 30 years and four movies later. "The guys that wear hats are a little bit sure of themselves.

It's a statement, you know. And before you make a statement, you want to make sure you make a proper statement for your own individual style," said Rod Springer, senior hat consultant.

But J. J. Hat Center is about more than just hats. It is a real throwback to another time. It is one of those classic shops your grandparents talked about, a place where salesmen fuss over customers and make them feel like kings, if only for a couple of hours. The majority of the shop's salesmen have been working in the hat business for more than 20 years, and the shop really prides itself on its customer service. "We really want you to come in here and have a shopping experience that you're going to walk out and feel great about," said Williamson.

J. J. Hat Center's extra attention to service does not end with your purchase. It also cleans and restores hats, changes bands, and does monogramming. Most of these services are free, even if the hat was purchased elsewhere. Reshaping hats is one of its specialties; it is amazing what a little nip and tuck can do. A hat is first steamed with a hand steamer, which softens the material and helps to draw out any dirt or stains. Next, while the hat is still moist, it is shaped and sculpted into the desired style—whether the brim is pulled up to create a less formal look or given a curved shape to add a little flair.

These days, it takes a special kind of person to wear a classic hat. Simply putting one on can transform you—don a fedora to feel a little more polished or a newsboy cap to feel a little more scrappy. "I wear a hat every day," said Jose Heriquez, another senior hat consultant. "No one is looking at me, but I know that I'm being noticed. And it's kind of cool, you know. Men that wear hats walk a little bit differently. They carry themselves a little bit differently. It's a statement."

J. J. HAT CENTER

Established in 1911

310 Fifth Avenue
Midtown, Manhattan
www.jjhatcenter.com
212-239-4368
Subway: N, Q, or R train to
34th Street–Herald Square
Open Monday–Friday:
9:00 a.m. to 6:00 p.m.
Saturday: 9:30 a.m. to 5:30 p.m.

JOHN'S OF
12TH STREET

Established in 1908

302 East 12th Street, East Village, Manhattan
www.johnsof12thstreet.com 212-475-9531
Subway: 4, 5, 6, L, N, Q, R, or W train to
14th Street–Union Square; L train to First Avenue
Open Monday–Thursday: 4:00 p.m. to 11:00 p.m.
Friday–Saturday: 4:00 p.m. to 11:30 p.m.
Sunday: 3:30 p.m. to 10:30 p.m.

Yes, Italian restaurants in New York City are a dime a dozen, but just try finding one with the same history, great stories, and fine food that makes John's of 12th Street so unique. It is a place that screams classic old Italian while meshing well with its hip and eclectic East Village home.

Way before the beatniks, hippies, punks, and hipsters staked their claim in the East Village, back when this area was a thriving European immigrant enclave, John's of 12th Street was here. Now one of the last holdouts of that long ago era, the restaurant is tucked away on one of the few quiet streets in the East Village. Its facade looks comfortably ensconced in its surroundings, as if quietly observing the neighborhood's ever-evolving look and feel.

Opened in 1908, John's looks almost the same today as it did then. All its classic fixtures are intact, like ornate floor tiles imported from Belgium and oversized red leather banquettes. There are unique touches, like the lower half of the walls, which are veneered with marble and stone, and the upper half of the walls, which are lined with murals of Italian landscapes. And don't forget the sharply dressed waiters warmly waiting on patrons.

Amazingly, as old as John's is, it has only had three owners in its history. The first was John Pucciatti, an Italian immigrant and a restaurateur by trade, and also an activist, to put it mildly. Pucciatti was a member of the notorious turn-of-the-century anarchist movement. Movement leaders like Carlo Tresca and Emma Goldman met and ate here regularly, no doubt planning many of their famous protests in nearby Union Square. And this was not Pucciatti's only nefarious activity. During Prohibition, he ran a speakeasy upstairs, serving gin in espresso cups while his wife dutifully made the hooch in the backyard still. Today, one can still see the faint impression of the speakeasy entrance in the hallway, now covered with plaster.

The restaurant's most curious piece is in the back dining room, where there is a little table with several candles sitting on a large mound of melted wax. The story goes that Pucciatti blew the candles out the day Prohibition began and did not relight them until it ended. Now, the candles are lit every evening in honor of the liberated libations. This little tradition has caused generations of candle wax build-up, causing the group of candles to look curiously like a miniature frozen waterfall.

John's son, Danny Pucciatti, eventually took over and ran the place as a respectable little Italian restaurant. Then, in 1972, he sold it to Mike Alpert and Nick Sitnycky, who have been here ever since. It is their appreciation of history and tradition that has kept this place a gem. They keep the place up-to-date, but with careful attention to preserving the original feel. For example, they repaired the vintage enameled refrigerator next to the bar instead of just replacing it.

That respect for tradition also shows in the restaurant's menu, which includes classic Italian fare like lasagna, spaghetti, and fettuccine. It also makes a mean Tuscan meat sauce, and much of its pasta is made in-house. One of its more unusual dishes is Spiedini alla Romana, an old Italian dish very few restaurants still serve. (Considering its gut-busting ingredients, that's probably a good thing.) Bread and mozzarella cheese are put on a skewer, drenched in flour and egg, and sauteed. It is then baked in the oven and topped with an anchovy and butter sauce. "It's not something your doctor would want you to eat every week, but it certainly is worth the calories," said Alpert.

With this being the East Village, John's of 12th Street also knows how to keep its menu up-to-date with the neighborhood. It offers quite a large vegan menu, substituting many of the meat selections with its own wheat gluten counterparts. It even makes its own vegan cannolis with coconut and cashew cream.

Over the years the restaurant has racked up its fair share of dining celebrities. Its brushes with greatness include Humphrey Bogart, Christopher Plummer, Robert DeNiro, Danny Kaye, Tom Cruise, and Jackie Kennedy, just to name a few. And yes, even a few mobsters have dined here,

including Lucky Luciano. According to Alpert, the celebrity experiences have been quite fun. One time, instead of telling the owners who he was, Tom Cruise waited patiently for a table. Co-owner Sitnycky didn't recognize him, even after asking Cruise to spell his name. Then there was the time Robert DeNiro forgot a stack of newspapers he brought to read while dining. Upon closer inspection, Alpert noticed the papers all had stories about Jake Lamotta. Apparently, DeNiro was researching his role for *Raging Bull*. Alpert later returned the papers to a very appreciative DeNiro. The Who guitarist Pete Townshend once dined here with Des McAnuff, the director of *Tommy*, to discuss the show. And last, but certainly not least, one of Alpert's fondest memories involved actor Christian Slater when he was a child. "His mother is casting director Mary Jo Slater and she managed to get Mark Hamill from *Star Wars* to come to his birthday party here," said Alpert. "He was totally surprised. You could tell he was a big *Star Wars* fan."

All the celebrities aside, Alpert enjoys and strives to make this restaurant a place where everyone feels welcome. One of the things he enjoys most about the neighborhood is the diversity it brings into the restaurant. "We have such a wide variety of customers that the contrast between them is sometimes like night and day, but there is no conflict and everybody enjoys themselves," said Alpert.

Julius Cohen

JEWELER

New York City is a likely contender for the jewelry capital of the world. Tiffany, Harry Winston, and Cartier are just some of the "mom-and-pop" jewelry stores in the Big Apple. But very few jewelry stores actually custom-make their own pieces in-house. Behold Julius Cohen Jeweler, makers of diamond and gold dreams.

Since 1956, this boutique jeweler has created custom-made jewelry for individual clients. Anyone can come in with an idea or design for a particular piece—be it a wedding ring, necklace, or brooch—and Julius Cohen will walk the customer through every step of the process. "I always say that I sell with my ears, not with my mouth, because you really have to be able to listen to what your customer is saying and interpret what they want," said owner Leslie Steinweiss. "But I'll never make anything that I don't love, so the aesthetic is always there, too."

Julius Cohen Jeweler is named after its founder, who started in the jewelry business at age 16 by apprenticing with his uncles at Oscar Heyman and Brothers. Later, he worked for Harry Winston, becoming one of its best salesmen. Having a desire to design his own jewelry and wanting to provide more one-on-one service, Cohen decided to open his own shop in 1956. He worked there until his death in 1995. Today, his son-in-law, Leslie Steinweiss—along with Leslie's wife, Marjory, and daughter, Parsley—carries on the family business. Another family member is also sometimes seen running around the place: Pinto the Chihuahua. More of a showroom model than a guard dog, she occasionally models necklaces to entertain visitors.

The shop's dedication to custom work lends itself to greater creativity and spontaneity in its pieces, which often have a whimsical feel. For instance, one of its signature pieces is a gold ring contoured like a saddle, which is often bought by horse enthusiasts. Another trademarked piece uses different shaped stones to spell out "hope" in accordance to their cuts (H for heart, O for oval, P for pear, and E for emerald). One of the more popular pieces is the barrel roll bracelet, which uses small barrel pieces encrusted with diamonds around the diameters. The bracelet moves easily along the wearer's arm, giving a sparkly effect, or, as the shop calls it, the "flash and roll." Parsley Steinweiss has recently given her grandfather's design a third-generational twist by incorporating the original barrel design into a ring and adding multicolored stones to the mix.

Along with its custom work, Julius Cohen is also well respected for some of its jewelry design innovations. For instance, it often takes ancient techniques and designs and incorporates them into modern jewelry. It was one of the first modern jewelers to incorporate traditional Indian-cut stones called briolettes—oval-shaped gems cut in triangular facets. Using natural-colored diamonds in its designs is another one of its innovations.

And if the shop's custom jewelry doesn't impress you, its one-of-a-kind object decor pieces will stop you in your tracks. For example, the functional miniature horse carousel standing just five inches high. Another favorite is a lapis and 22-carat gold domino set complete with a fitted box.

It should not be surprising that many Julius Cohen customers include the rich and famous, but as part of the store's policy, it won't name names. One person who was open about her purchases was the actress Greer Garson. She bought several pieces from then-owner Julius Cohen over the years, playfully nicknaming him "Sparkle Plenty."

But Julius Cohen Jeweler also has a certain appreciation when it is able to design something for those of us with a more conservative budget. "Sometimes people are intimidated by our history. Custom work in itself requires a certain amount of time and can get quite costly, but we've also been able to make an engagement ring for $2,500. We love doing what we're doing and I think that almost any pocketbook would be happy," said Steinweiss. No matter what the final price, it is important to Julius Cohen that a client is completely happy with his or her purchase. "It becomes a part of you, a part of your everyday life. That's the incredible thing about jewelry. It's so intimate," said Steinweiss.

JULIUS COHEN JEWELER

Established in 1956

699 Madison Avenue
Upper East Side, Manhattan
www.juliuscohen.com
212-371-3050
Subway: N, Q, or R train to
Fifth Avenue–59th Street
Open by appointment only.

The picture frame. One might think of it as an afterthought to a work of art, but it is so much more. A proper frame not only complements a painting, but also makes it unforgettable. In fact, some established artists are known to choose a frame for a painting before they even pick up the brush. One place in New York City understands the importance of framing. It's Julius Lowy Frame and Restoring Company, caretakers of some of the most prized works of art in the world.

Located in a stately brownstone on the Upper East Side, the craftspersons at Julius Lowy work to return priceless pieces of art to their former glory. "We sort of consider ourselves picture doctors," said co-owner Larry Shar. "We do pretty much anything that a collector, art dealer, or artist might need for their paintings."

With six floors of space—each devoted to its own specialty, be it gilding, framing, or restoration—Julius Lowy is the oldest and one of the largest fine arts service firms in the world, not to mention one of the oldest businesses in New York City.

It was founded in 1907 by Julius Lowy. Shar's father, Hilly, started working at the store as a teenager in the 1920s. Gradually, he learned restoration techniques and eventually bought the business. Like his father, Shar joined the business as a young man. "After school it was a choice of becoming a rock musician or making a living, so I opted for the latter and I guess the rest is history," he said. "I've been doing it for the last 40 years."

Now his son, Brad, and daughter, Tracy, have joined the business. "It's very heartwarming to walk into work every day and know that you have the support of your family, particularly your offspring," said Shar. "I was fortunate enough to have had a fabulous mentor in my father. It's a lifelong dream to be able to have that kind of relationship with my son and with my daughter."

Not surprisingly, Julius Lowy's clients are a who's who of the fine art world, including collectors like the Rockefeller and Getty families, auction houses like Sotheby's and Christie's, and even artists like Salvador Dali.

Julius Lowy has cared for some of the best-known images in the world, including Cézanne's *The Bathers* and Van Gogh's *Portrait of the Postman Joseph Roulin*. "I can remember being a young kid and coming into my father's offices and seeing a Monet and a Cézanne hanging around," said Brad Shar. "There's always a Picasso hanging around here or there, so famous artists have just been part of my daily language."

Julius Lowy's relationship with a painting begins with its conservation, which includes cleaning the painting, removing old varnish, readjusting the canvas, and carefully touching up scratches, cracks, and missing paint. Like any proper restoration company, Julius Lowy uses only materials and techniques that are reversible. This is done so that future restorers—perhaps with better technology—may be able to restore the painting even further. "It is detective work," said conservator Lauren Rich. "I mean, every painting has its own story, and there are certain tools you can use to figure out that story."

But conservation is just part of the Julius Lowy story. The shop also has an expert framing department, with some 5,000 antique frames that range from around the 16th century up through the early 20th century. It very likely has the largest such inventory in the world. Prices range from $5,000 to $250,000. Julius Lowy can also make reproductions of antique frames (including hand-gilding) and design new frames for collectors and artists alike.

Even with all these great works of art coming in and out of its doors, it's important for people know that Julius Lowy is truly full service. "I'd like people to understand that despite the fact that we do deal with Monets and Picassos on a daily basis, people should not feel intimidated to walk into Lowy, because a great deal of the work we do is with paintings that have sentimental value, that are meaningful to people in the neighborhood, whether it be ancestral portraits or even photographs of their children."

JULIUS LOWY FRAME AND RESTORING COMPANY

Established in 1907

223 East 80th Street
Upper East Side, Manhattan
212-861-8585 www.lowyonline.com
Subway: 4 or 6 train to 77th Street
Open Monday–Friday:
9:00 a.m. to 5:30 p.m.

CURTAIN ORNAMENTS
AND BRACKETS
Made to order,
OLD FRAMES
REGILT.

KEENS STEAKHOU

Keens
STEAKHOUSE

PRESIDENT LINCOLN
BENEFIT
LAST NIGHT
LAURA KEENE

ONE THOUSAND NIGHTS
OUR AMERICAN
COUSIN

KEENS STEAKHOUSE

Established in 1885

72 West 36th Street
Herald Square, Manhattan
www.keens.com 212-947-3636
Subway: B, D, F, M, N, Q, or R train
to 34th Street–Herald Square
Open Monday–Friday: 11:45 a.m. to 10:30 p.m.
Saturday: 5:00 p.m. to 10:30 p.m.
Sunday: 5:00 p.m. to 9:00 p.m.

Lifelong New Yorkers are often surprised when they find out about Keens Steakhouse. How could a place with such a unique history and a great reputation for steaks not be on their radar? Perhaps Keens itself is partially to blame, for it simply concentrates on its patrons having a great dining experience rather than angling to make top ten lists or making sure the right celebrities eat there.

"Every restaurant sort of has its niche. We're seen as the earnest, hardworking steakhouse that's been around for a long time. We're genuine and we treat people the way we'd like to be treated," said general manager Bonnie Jenkins.

Located in Herald Square, Keens is the oldest steakhouse in New York City. It opened in 1885 and is the lone survivor of when the neighborhood was America's premier theater district. In the 19th century, iconic theaters like the Garrick, Globe, and the old Metropolitan Opera lined the streets. Actors from around the world came to perform, many from the famed theaters of London. Many of them were members of The Lamb's Club, a popular social club for theater folk. Often feeling homesick, the members decided to open up a Lamb's Club branch in New York, which still exists today and is now in Times Square. Restaurateur Albert Keens was sent to America with the task of putting the club's headquarters in the restaurant that bears his name. The restaurant

immediately became popular as *the* place to be before and after performances for both theatergoers and performers. Even when the theater district moved uptown, Keens held on as a reliable place for steaks.

The restaurant takes up three nondescript brownstones on 36th Street. Inside are a myriad of rooms and spaces with their own distinctive looks and themes, but one thing takes center stage—the restaurant's staggering collection of churchwarden pipes. Nearly 90,000 of these pipes are hung on the ceiling and in several display cases.

"The tradition of churchwarden pipes goes back to the days of old English taverns. Popular for their very mild and smooth smoke, the pipes are made of soft clay and have a long stem. Not surprisingly, they did not travel well so it became customary for taverns to hold their patrons' pipes," said Keens maître d' and historian, James Conley. Keens dutifully carried on this tradition for decades, even employing a pipe warden to archive and care for the pipes. Pipes owned by Babe Ruth, General Douglas MacArthur, and J. P. Morgan are in the collection. Recent additions include Tom Hanks and Chuck Norris.

Due to changing tastes and a citywide ban on smoking in public places, it has been years since any of the pipes have been smoked. Still, people regularly stop in looking for their grandfather's or great-grandfather's pipe. On occasion, Keens is able to reunite the family with the pipe, thanks to its cataloging system. The tradition is to snap the pipe in half once its owner passes away.

During the 1970s, Keens went through a rough patch—as did the rest of the city—and eventually closed its doors. Luckily, George and Kiki Schwarz happened to walk by one day. Peering inside the darkened windows, they were immediately inspired to buy Keens and bring it back to its original glory. Initially thinking it would take just weeks to get the place back in shape, it in reality took three years and more than a million dollars. Whole floors and walls had to be reconstructed and the kitchen was fully modernized. Workers even chiseled out a new basement to make room for a wine cellar and dry aging room for the steaks.

Thankfully, even after the restoration, today's patrons will find few changes since their ancestors first dined here. The decor hasn't changed—there are countless wall decorations, paintings, and photographs; original political cartoons from the pages of *Punch* and *Harper's*; and vintage theater playbills, including one from Buffalo Bill's Wild West show. The pub room, with its hearty old oak tables and chairs and deep rich wood paneling, offers customers a more casual setting than the main dining room. Like many modern sports pubs, there are original photographs and clippings of local sports heroes, but these heroes are more than a century old, with names like Walter Johnson, Hughie Jennings, and Ty Cobb. And you can't miss "Ms. Keens," an enormous painting behind the bar. It depicts a reclining nude woman rumored to have been modeled after a Ziegfeld girl in the 1910s.

In the upstairs dining area, customers can still sit where The Lamb's Club used to meet after a night of performing. Sepia-toned photographs of past members line the wall. One room upstairs, the Lillie Langtry Room, is named after an actress who was rumored to be the mistress of King Edward VII. In 1905, she sued Keens because women were refused service. The restaurant eventually relented, though

only halfway—it allowed women to dine in separate rooms from the men. "When I came here in 1997, there was still a lot of testosterone here. Now, women run Keens, so it's a neat thing to see how the world changes," said Jenkins.

For those who love history, the Lincoln Room does not disappoint. It is filled with pictures and memorabilia of the 16th president, including a copy of the Gettysburg Address handwritten by Lincoln himself. The most astonishing artifact by far is an original program from the play *Our American Cousin*, which Lincoln was attending when John Wilkes Booth shot him on April 14, 1865. It is said that Lincoln was holding this very program at the moment of his death. There are even dark splotches on the program rumored to be Lincoln's own blood.

All of these interesting artifacts aside, Keens does not rest on its laurels as simply a historic New York City restaurant. This is a real chophouse with a national reputation as one of New York City's best places for steaks. The restaurant takes particular pride in its USDA-certified meats, which are hand-selected by the restaurant's meat steward. The restaurant then dry ages select cuts on the premises and regularly researches meat suppliers and farms across the country. Keens is also well-known for its mutton chop. For the uninitiated, this is a saddle cut of a one-year-old lamb. It is known for its very moist, tender, and succulent taste. Back in 1935, Keens sold its one-millionth mutton chop to great fanfare.

In addition to the delicious food, the restaurant also has a reputation for single malt scotch. The bar serves some 300 different bottlings. Public tastings are held regularly to give patrons a taste of the fine art of single malt scotch.

All of this together—the history, the decor, the delicious food and drinks—ensures that Keens stays on top of the New York City steakhouse game. "People have a choice. They can go to a million different restaurants in New York City," said Jenkins. "So when people choose this restaurant, we're really grateful for that. We hope this restaurant is still going 100 years from now."

Mario Cuomo

Elliot Gould

Spencer Christian

Jonathan Demme

Robert F. Wagner

Chuck Norris

KENNY'S CASTAWAYS

Established in 1967

157 Bleecker Street
Greenwich Village, Manhattan
www.kennyscastaways.net
917-475-1323
Subway: A, C, E, B, D, F, or M train
to West Fourth Street
Open daily from 12:00 p.m. to 4:00 a.m.

There is that old saying that rock-and-roll will never die. It is certainly true down on Greenwich Village's Bleecker Street, for it is the clubs along this street that have been helping new artists get noticed in New York City for the past 50 years. Kenny's Castaways is one such place, an original rock club that still to this day gives bands a place to hone their skills and become rock stars.

It must be doing something right, for Kenny's alumni is represented all over the club's walls in the form of mementos that would make even the Hard Rock Café envious—vintage albums, signed guitars, and original photographs of music legends before they hit it big. "It's like in the theater district, where everybody has done *Cats*," said co-owner Maria Kenny. "Well, in New York everybody wants to play Kenny's at some point because that's where the musical history is. We really want to foster talent in people. We want to help develop people in whatever way we can. Most places are not able to do that. I'm just grateful that we can."

The club's inception began in 1967, when Maria's father, Patrick Kenny, opened a bar on Manhattan's Upper East Side. Wanting to get closer to the downtown music scene, he decided to "castaway" and created this Bleecker Street spot in 1975. He wanted it to be a place where burgeoning talent could play, without all the usual red tape

and regardless of their connections. Patrick Kenny would often see people performing on the street, and if they were good enough, he would invite them in to play on the stage.

Surely he knew what he was doing, for some of the greatest bands in history can trace their origins to his club. Phish, Bonnie Raitt, Rod Stewart, Aerosmith, and the Fugees are just some of many talented artists that have graced the club's stage. The New York Dolls played at Kenny's, and from one of those shows the Ramones were formed (Joey met Dee Dee at a show). And way before the makeup, Kiss members Gene Simmons and Paul Stanley performed at the club in an early incarnation of the band.

One band in particular has a special place in the history of Kenny's Castaways—The Smithereens. Patrick Kenny took the band under his wing when they were first starting out, even giving lead singer Pat Dinizio a day job before the band hit it big. "Pat Kenny was our mentor in New York, and he booked us here all the time," said drummer Dennis Diken. "We became a de facto house band, really. He was a great supporter of us and a great friend, and a real spiritual father to us."

Another favorite who went on to a few bigger things is Bruce Springsteen. "He did a one-week gig here, because, according to my father, he couldn't get a gig in Manhattan to get record people to notice him," said co-owner Thomas Kenny. "He was a Jersey artist, and back then, the talent agencies wouldn't travel to New Jersey. After his first performance, he turned to my father, and said, 'So I did OK?' and my father said, 'You did OK, kid.'" And Springsteen got more than one of his first big breaks here. On occasion, he would come in to listen to other bands. One night he met the host of the Monday Midnight Jam—Patti Scialfa. Several years later, he married her.

With all those legends coming through over the years, there are plenty of great stories. Thomas Kenny remembers one night in particular. "Yoko Ono was the first concert my father brought me down here to see. Let me tell you, I was not impressed. I was a 12-year-old and there she was up on stage wearing some kind of underwear garment and a bra. She took off part of her underwear garment, threw it out into the crowd, and dared the guys to try it on. I said to my father, 'This is music?' He smiled and said, 'One day you'll understand.'"

Its rock-and-roll history aside, the location itself has had quite a journey. It is a rare Federal-style building dating back to at least the 1820s—one of very few left in New York City. Historians believe it has always been a bar or restaurant,

among other things. It has a past that would make even the most decadent rock-and-roller blush (or perhaps fit right in!). In the 1890s, owner Frank Stevenson turned it into a bar called The Slide, which the *New York Herald* and *New York Press* called "the den of iniquity" because it was the first openly gay bar in New York City. At some point, the club was also a brothel and speakeasy. The numerous small rooms in the basement hint at prostitution. In fact, during recent renovations, Maria and Thomas Kenny discovered wallboards in the basement with writing that said things like "Large Woman, 50 Cents; Sheets This Way." Dozens of Prohibition-era bottles were also discovered between the walls, some with their labels still attached.

Today, Kenny's continues to open its doors to new talent. Prospective performers only have to send in a demo CD to be considered. Big names still perform here, too, so don't be surprised if you stumble upon one of their impromptu jams. (Ben Harper is one big-league performer who enjoys using Kenny's as a place to try out new material.) Though Patrick Kenny died in 2002, his family continues his legacy. His wife, daughter, and three sons all pitch in, making sure this New York City rock-and-roll club remains a family-run business. Surely that would make him proud.

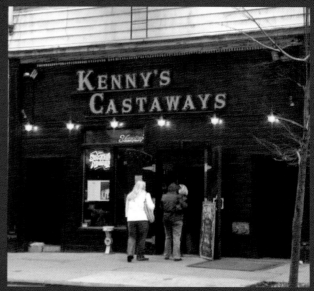

New York City is a neon lover's dream. There is probably more of it in the Big Apple than anywhere else in the world; Times Square alone is practically wrapped in neon tubing. But someone has to create and repair all these neon signs. That is where the folks at Let There Be Neon come in.

This venerable workshop and studio has been plying its craft since 1972. It is not only one of the last neon manufacturers left in the city, but also one of the only craftsmen's shops remaining in the once-industrial neighborhood of Tribeca. Housed in an old cast-iron building, Let There Be Neon's vibrant neon-drenched storefront casts a splashy hue on an otherwise monotone neighborhood. Inside the studio, neon artisans create one-of-a-kind works of art, and also repair and restore the classic signs of New York City.

Let There Be Neon was the brainchild of the late contemporary artist Rudi Stern, who helped elevate neon into a serious art form and even wrote four books on the subject. Over the years, Stern designed neon for theater, opera, television, and film productions, and even for rock groups like The Byrds and The Doors. "Rudi was always in love with the beauty of neon," said current owner Jeff Friedman.

The studio's clients run the gamut—from pizza parlors to Bloomingdale's and everything in between, including numerous contemporary artists. With some 50 colors in the neon pallet, the art is quite flexible, both practically and artistically. Neon lighting can last up to 50 years and is quite energy-efficient. The shop also rents neon signs for Broadway, film, and television, many of which are creatively displayed in the front gallery of the studio, which is open to the public.

Neon was first used in advertising in 1912 in Paris, France. The United States followed in 1923, when neon was used to advertise automobiles at a Los Angeles dealership. Neon hit its stride after Prohibition, when bar owners found it to be effective advertising for their recently liberated libations. It did see decline in the 1950s and '60s, due to changing tastes and the advent of cheap plastic fluorescent signs. But lately neon has made a comeback, particularly in New York City. Times Square even has an ordinance requiring all storefronts to have at least one neon sign.

"It just has a strong identity in and of itself and that filters through the environment," said artist Ross Muir. "You just feel it has its own personality. For a light source to have a personality is not too common, so neon does have that."

The process of creating neon has changed very little over the decades. All neon must be custom-made by hand. First, a paper pattern is made. A glass tube is then marked at the points where it needs to bend to coincide with the pattern. Next, the neon-maker heats the glass with a gas burner until it melts so that it has a consistency similar to a firm rubber tube. Then, the tube is pulled out of the fire, laid on the pattern, and shaped to the correct measurements before it hardens again. During all of this, the neon-maker occasionally blows into the tube to help it keep its shape. Once the tube is the correct shape, it is hooked up to a vacuum pump and the air inside is replaced with either neon or argon gas. Electrodes are attached to the tubes and the gas inside is charged with electricity, creating the glow so familiar with neon. Then, it's ready to be added to the New York landscape.

As long as New Yorkers love their neon, Let There Be Neon will continue to provide them with this magic light. "We're really proud of our company. We believe we've helped neon retain its visibility through the years," said Friedman.

LET THERE BE NEON

Established in 1972

38 White Street, Tribeca, Manhattan
www.lettherebeneon.com
212-226-4883
Subway: A, C, or E train
to Canal Street
Open Monday–Friday:
9:00 a.m. to 5:00 p.m.

LEXINGTON CANDY SHOP

Established in 1925

1226 Lexington Avenue
Upper East Side, Manhattan
www.lexingtoncandyshop.com
212-288-0057
Subway: 4, 5, or 6 train to 86th Street
Open Monday–Saturday:
7:00 a.m. to 7:00 p.m.
Sunday: 8:00 a.m. to 6:00 p.m.

They were once as common and indispensable to New Yorkers as the corner deli or street cart. The humble luncheonette was a place where hardworking New Yorkers could grab a quick meal and maybe a little conversation. Today, soup stands, salad joints, and gourmet coffee shops rule the city streets where these places once stood. But thankfully, a few luncheonettes have managed to stick around, including Lexington Candy Shop, located on the Upper East Side.

Lexington Candy Shop was first opened in 1925 by third-generation co-owner John Philis's grandfather, Soterios Philis, a Greek immigrant. His son, Pete, soon joined the business and ran it for several years. Then, in 1980, John came in and has been there ever since. More recently, Robert Karcher joined the business as co-owner after years in the fast-food business. He helps to keep the place competitive with chain stores.

Lexington Candy Shop's name might be a little confusing to some people. Actually, very little candy is sold here. The name comes from a time when the place devoted half of its space to candy making and chocolates. Though it switched to an all-luncheonette business in 1948, John Philis's father felt it was too late to change the name. Today, people still come in looking for candy. Visitors are rarely disappointed, though. Instead of candy, they find a menu that offers classic American fare—burgers, fries, chicken salad, grilled cheese, roast beef, and turkey. To keep up with the some of the more trendy lunch places popping up in Manhattan, Lexington offers some contemporary fare, like Greek and Caesar salads and veggie and turkey burgers. "We have adjusted a little bit, but we haven't gone too far out of our niche," said Philis.

In addition to the delicious lunch menu, Lexington serves classic soda fountain drinks made the old-fashioned way. These include malts that use real malted powder, not liquid, which many places use these days in order to skimp. Milkshakes are made with the restaurant's own homemade syrups and Bassetts ice cream, which is known for its high butter fat content. (Lexington is one of the few places in New York City selling the brand.) Then there is the restaurant's specialty—classic freshly squeezed lemonade. Even the Coca-Cola is better here. It is made to order: a couple of squirts of cola syrup, some carbonated water, and then a quick stir. And let us not forget the old New York standard: egg creams. Lexington has a bit of an edge over the competition, for it makes its own chocolate syrup, giving the creams a fresher and richer taste.

According to Philis, Lexington is a real neighborhood place. "We have a nice crowd of regulars. When we see

them coming, we start their order. We are all creatures of habit, myself included," said Philis. And so is Lexington Candy Shop, for it has changed very little over the decades. Most of the interior hasn't been updated since 1948. Rather, it has been carefully kept up and maintained. There are dark wood booths, old glass cabinets, and—of course— a classic lunch counter complete with stainless-steel stools and a soda fountain.

Men dressed in traditional soda jerk uniforms work the fountain, frying eggs and making sweet drinks with vintage equipment—including gas-fired coffee urns, still making great coffee after more than 65 years of service; prewar sea-foam-green drink mixers; and even an orange juicer that has been around since 1940. "Things break down from time-to-time and that's always an adventure, finding spare parts," said Philis. "When we replaced the original drink mixer, people got upset, so we had to go back and repair the original one. They may be right, however; the old one does make a better milkshake."

The vintage fixtures are not the only visual treats in this place. One cannot help but notice Philis's enormous collection of Coca-Cola bottles and collectibles, which are tucked in every possible space. Customers have even brought Philis bottles from as far away as Egypt and China. "It's nice," he said. "They don't want anything for it, just the satisfaction of me putting it in the window."

Lexington Candy Shop's authentic interior has not been lost on the media. According to Philis, around three dozen magazine advertisements and commercials have been shot here, including ads for Brooks Brothers, Mercedes, and Playtex Bras. A few movies have also been shot here, including *The Nanny Diaries* starring Scarlett Johansson and *Three Days of the Condor* starring Robert Redford. The latter is Philis's personal favorite. Why? "During the scene when Redford comes into the place, you can see me in the back yelling 'Chicken Plate!'" he said. In addition to the movie shoots, the restaurant has had its fair share of celebrities coming in just for a bite to eat, including Bruce Springsteen, Ben Stiller, and Uma Thurman, among others. Paul McCartney has been a regular for 40 years.

Lexington Candy Shop also hosts special events and private parties. During these events, guests are allowed to get behind the counter and make their own sundaes and fountain drinks. Parties have included wedding rehearsals, graduations, book releases, and—of course—birthday parties.

"This is not the easiest way to make a living, but there is a sense of pride, there is a sense of history," said Philis. "You want to continue something like this; you don't want to just let it disappear. It does get more difficult every year— especially when it comes to finding parts to fix our vintage equipment—but we truly try our best, and so far, it seems to be working."

NOM WAH TEA PARLOR

Established in 1920

13 Doyers Street, Chinatown, Manhattan
www.nomwah.com 212-962-6047
Subway: 6, J, M, N, Q, R, W, or Z train
to Canal Street
Open daily 10:30 a.m. to 9:00 p.m.

Some say the youth have little appreciation for tradition and longevity, but that's certainly not so at one restaurant in Chinatown, where—thanks to the younger generation—a historic spot has a new lease on life.

It is Nom Wah Tea Parlor, the first and oldest dim sum restaurant in Chinatown. The restaurant is located on Doyers Street, which itself has been front and center during much of Chinatown's history. Known as "Bloody Angle," Doyers Street was the scene of dozens of murders in the 19th and early 20th centuries. The street's unusual sharp angles made for a perfect place for rival gangs to surprise and sabotage each other. In fact, it is said that more murders have happened on Doyers Street than any other street in New York City.

Nom Wah Tea Parlor surely witnessed some of this dangerous history, for it first opened at this location as a bakery and tea parlor in 1920. For decades, it served the neighborhood as a reliable place for locals. In 1974, the owners, the Choy family, sold the business to one of their employees, Wally Tang, who had been working there since the 1950s. Then, in 2010, he decided to retire at the age of 80. Not wanting to completely let go of the place, he offered his thirtysomething nephew, Wilson Tang, a partnership in order to keep the place going.

Wilson Tang's first mission was to give Nom Wah Tea Parlor a spit shine without destroying its patina and nostalgic charm. For instance, he repaired, rather than replaced, the classic blood-red banquettes that have defined the dining space for decades. He also kept vintage stainless-steel kitchen implements, like the gigantic gas-fired coffee brewers and steamer boxes behind the luncheon counter. "I like the fact that every time my uncle walks in, it looks the same," said Tang. "He is still able to sit, eat, and reminisce over the fruits of his labor." There is only one modern update: a big flat-screen television in the dining area.

Tang's efforts have resulted in one of the best-preserved prewar-era interiors in the city. It is a place dying to be compared to an Edward Hopper painting or film noir movie set. Remnants of eras past are all over the place—the Victorian tin ceiling; the Art Deco post moldings; the 1950s-era luncheon counter; the antique teacups. The shop's vintage enameled metal sign is one of the last of its kind in Chinatown; it is a beacon of classic New York City in the otherwise banal storefront landscape of vinyl and plastic signs that now plagues the neighborhood.

Restoring the restaurant was only half the work. Tang spent as much energy on the menu, carefully updating it for newcomers while keeping it authentic for longtime regulars.

This is not an easy task in New York City, considering that everyone from college students to cab drivers knows good dim sum. For the uninitiated, dim sum is simply a variety of small dishes of food to sample and share. The tradition dates back to the Silk Road in China, when travelers would stop along the way for different kinds of food. The name "dim sum" translates to "a touch of heart," meaning it is made from the heart. It is not an easy discipline to master; dim sum chefs spend decades working on their accreditation.

Today, Nom Wah Tea Parlor offers more than 50 menu items, such as spare ribs, sticky rice with Chinese sausage, roast pork buns, and several varieties of dumplings. All of the menu items are printed on a paper checklist with full descriptions in both English and Chinese; the list even indicates which items are vegetarian or gluten-free. One of its standouts is its traditional egg roll. Most people have never had a "real" egg roll due to the amount of work involved. Many restaurants skimp by using a processed premade egg roll wrapper. A true egg roll is made with real eggs. A crepe is made first, and then the filling is rolled in. All of it is then battered and fried. "The result is actually a very moist, aromatic, and fresh egg roll," said Tang. To finish off the

meal, customers can try the restaurant's signature dessert: almond cookies, which are displayed proudly under a cake cover on the counter.

Every day Nom Wah Tea Parlor hosts longtime locals, as well as tour groups from all over America and Europe, who are looking for an authentic Chinatown dining experience. It is one of those rare places that can balance accessibility with not losing its soul or authenticity. And this authenticity has not been lost on filmmakers. Movies like *Reversal of Fortune* and *Spiderman* have had scenes shot here, as well as numerous episodes of the television show *Law and Order*. Director Woody Allen even frequented the place; he shot a scene from his movie *Radio Days* here.

Now, if only Tang could convince his parents. "Well, being second-generation Chinese in America, my parents strived and worked really hard when they first came here to make sure that I wouldn't have to. I fulfilled my end of the bargain, graduating college with a degree in business economics and working for Morgan Stanley. But working for a big company was not really sitting well with me. My parents were really hesitant about me coming into this kind of business, but they're starting to come around."

OLD TOWN BAR
AND RESTAURANT

Established in 1892

45 East 18th Street
Flatiron District and Gramercy, Manhattan
www.oldtownbar.com 212-529-6732
Subway: N, Q, R, L, 4, 5, or 6 train
to Union Square
Open Monday–Thursday:
11:00 a.m. to 12:00 a.m.
Friday: 11:30 a.m. to 12:00 a.m.
Saturday: 12:00 p.m. to 1:00 a.m.
Sunday: 12:00 p.m. to 11:30 p.m.
Please note that the kitchen
is only open until 11:30 p.m.

Old Town Bar and Restaurant is one of those places New Yorkers find comfort in; as the city goes through its inevitable changes, this bar stays wondrously the same. This is in part thanks to two brothers, Gerard and Matthew Meagher, who carry on their father's tradition of the fine art of tavern keeping.

Every inch of Old Town is original and authentic, including the gaslight fixtures now converted to electricity, out-of-date separate entrances for men and women, beveled mirrors, the 17-foot ceiling with pressed tin, and the 90-foot mahogany bar that defines the space. Some of the booths still have seats that lift up; these were used to hide alcohol during Prohibition. Another interesting feature is the call buttons at the tables. "The buttons used to work," said co-owner Matthew Meagher. "The first couple of waitresses that worked here were driven crazy. Somewhere along the line we disconnected them. People thought that they would actually get service if they pressed the buttons, but, if anything, they would *not* get service by pressing the buttons."

First called Viemeister's, the tavern was built in 1892 by German immigrants and was one of several German restaurants in the neighborhood. Today, it is one of the last remnants of a once-thriving German community on 18th Street near Union Square. In 1933, Claus Lohden bought the restaurant and changed the name to Old Town. It passed through the decades rather quietly until the 1960s, when it began to fade along with the Union Square neighborhood. "You could count the people at the bar at 9 p.m., and it was usually closed by 10 p.m.," said Meagher. "You would get people like Andy Warhol, Bill Murray, and Keith Richards coming in, but you knew who they were because there was nobody else in the bar." After a series of owners, Matthew and Gerard's father, Larry Meagher, came into the business in the 1970s, and the bar started to regenerate.

Business was helped in the 1980s by an unlikely source: David Letterman. For years, Old Town's neon sign and bar interior were used in the opening shots of *Late Show with David Letterman*. According to Matthew Meagher, people

the OLD TOWN BAR
Congratulates
LIAM NEESON
"our best actor"

OLD TOWN
BAR
RESTAURANT

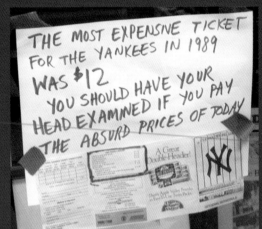

THE MOST EXPENSIVE TICKET FOR THE YANKEES IN 1989 WAS $12 YOU SHOULD HAVE YOUR HEAD EXAMINED IF YOU PAY THE ABSURD PRICES OF TODAY

A SHORT HISTORY OF THE OLD TOWN BAR RESTAURANT.

would often come by and ask if Letterman was there, and the employees would joke that he had just left. "I don't think he's ever been here," he said, chuckling.

The usage of the sign in the *Late Show* opening began a long relationship with the entertainment business. Several movies have been shot here—including *The Devil's Own*, *Bullets over Broadway*, and *The Last Days of Disco*—as well as commercials and even a Madonna music video. Some actors—like Tom Cruise and Liam Neeson—even found Old Town to be a great place to hang out. "We'd get a lot of celebrities because we were right near the Broadway rehearsal studios. We don't fawn over celebrities; we treat everybody the same, with respect. I think they like that democratic attitude," said co-owner Gerard Meagher.

Old Town is also literary mecca of sorts. Several writers have frequented it, including Jim Dwyer and Frank McCourt, whose book covers grace the walls.

Old Town doesn't rest on nostalgia or fame, though. It is a vibrant, working tavern, thanks to Gerard and Matthew, who take bar keeping to an almost scientific level. Conversation is so important here that the television is almost always on mute. Cell phone usage is banned. To help keep the conversation flowing, the brothers use one of their father's old tricks—posting short, handwritten editorials on the walls on just about any subject.

"We don't cater to drunks. We cater to interesting conversation," said Gerard Meagher. "We have a rotating cast of characters, which gives people a chance to meet somebody that they haven't met before. We also have New York people that work here, not actors just off the bus from Kansas, but real New Yorkers whose family history is here."

Old Town's food also stands up against any of the best restaurants in New York City. It serves hearty and fresh tavern food. "We make everything fresh. We make the potato salad raw, we cut our own French fries, we make our own coleslaw. Nothing comes out of an Ore-Ida bag; everything here is made right from scratch," said Gerard.

Old Town's best qualities—good food, good ambiance, and good conversation—continue decade after decade. "I know when I'm working and I can just hear people talking that things are going well," said Matthew. "If you just hear silence or if you hear too much music or if everyone's looking at the game, then you know that's not good for the overall atmosphere of the bar." Certainly, Larry Meagher would be proud of his boys.

In SoHo, there's a modest brick building with quite a few tales to tell. Since the 19th century, it has been used for several nefarious enterprises, all under the shadow of its local neighbor, the former New York City police headquarters. Without losing its edge, it is now a flip bistro called Onieal's.

As long as anyone can remember, the building at 174 Grand Street has been a tavern. It was built in 1875 and for years was known as the Newsroom Bar, becoming a de facto hangout for reporters. They would stake out the windows hoping to spot the next bigwig—someone like John Dillinger or Al Capone—getting booked across the street.

But there were also more dubious uses for the building. "It was hidden in plain sight as a speakeasy," said historian Jef Klein. "And, of course, the prostitution—everybody knew about it and they were participating in it so it was protected. It had friends in high places, let's put it that way." No one disputes that some of those friends in high places were right across the street. There was an underground tunnel connecting the tavern with the headquarters. Officially, it was used for transporting criminals to nearby horse stables, but it is rumored to have also been used for more recreational matters. Now bricked up, the tunnel is currently a wine cellar for Onieal's.

Decades came and went on Grand Street, and then in 1973 the police department moved uptown and the former headquarters was converted into luxury condos. As for the tavern, it lingered on for several years in different incarnations. In 1994, restaurateur Chris Onieal came in and completely reinvented the space.

His first order of business was restoring the building's famed carved wood ceiling, which is one of the most unique in the city. The ceiling is not original to the building

and its history is a bit fuzzy. It was built and installed in another establishment and thus could be much older than the building; it could have originated as far away as Europe. A mix of walnut, mahogany, and oak woods, several intricate details—like smiling devils and floral designs—are carved into it, giving it a regal but whimsical feel. "It dominated the space so much that my architect, Kate Webb, decided that we were going to just work with it," said Onieal. "We did an Edward Hopper kind of bar. I'm glad we did it, I like the feel of it, it feels like a hideaway."

That feeling may have been advantageous for some of Onieal's clientele. Several years ago, when he had that fatwa against him, Salmon Rushdie was coming in quite a bit. Onieal led the author to a table in front and left him alone. After realizing that Rushdie might be uncomfortable sitting in front of the window, he went back and said, "Mr. Rushdie, don't worry, I'm advertising and people still can't find me down here."

Luckily, customers did eventually find the restaurant. Onieal calls his menu progressive American, but it is always changing. "If I have a chef come in who has a French background, I will let him do three or four items that are representative of his cooking and then keep our standard pieces," said Onieal.

The ambiance and cuisine of Onieal's also caught the eye of *Sex and the City* producers, who ended up filming several episodes here, calling the bar Scout in the series. Bus tours now come by several times a week, bringing in fans who want to order a Cosmo, just like the *Sex and the City* girls. Hollywood stardom aside, though, Onieal would like his restaurant to be best known for one thing: "Reliability. I would like to go down as the most reliable place in New York. I think that's the most important thing."

ONIEAL'S

Established in 1994

174 Grand Street
SoHo, Manhattan
www.onieals.com
212-941-9119
Subway: 4, 5, or 6 train
to Spring Street
Open Sunday–Wednesday:
11:30 a.m. to 2:00 a.m.
Thursday–Saturday:
11:30 a.m. to 4:00 a.m.

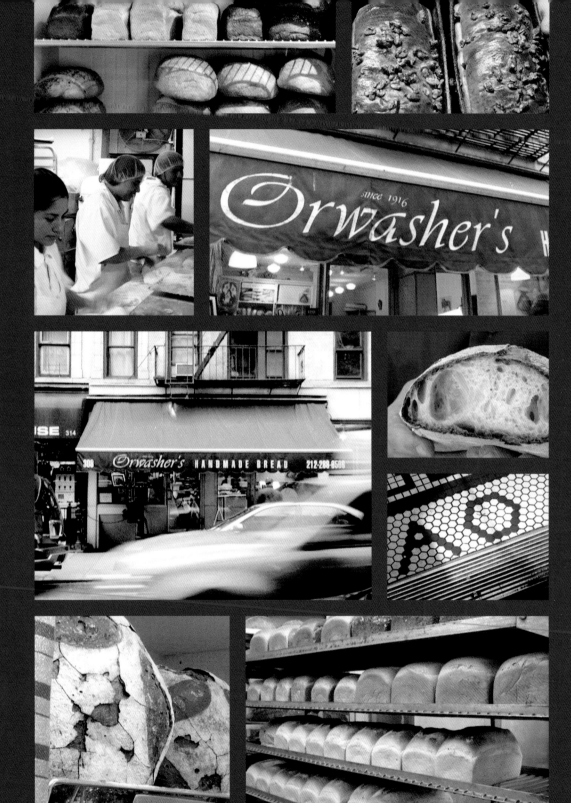

Yorkville on the Upper East Side was once one of the largest German and Hungarian neighborhoods in America, but looking around today one would never know it. Brownstones once jammed with immigrant families are now filled with young professionals trying to make it in the corporate world. Some of the old world is still around, though, including Orwasher's Bakery on East 78th Street, which has been perfecting the fine art of bread making since 1916.

"In New York City, as far as I know, there is not another bakery set up like this," said owner Keith Cohen. "This is very much reminiscent of the old European-style bakeries. You know supermarkets, they're great, but there's nothing like coming into a small bakery for a freshly baked product. You get to know everyone here, and you get to know the product. There's a certain romance about it."

Orwasher's Bakery could easily get by on its looks—the interior screams quaint old New York, from the ornate tiled floor to the cramped shelves packed with bread. But looks aside, this is a first-class bakery that supplies the Upper East Side with both classic and artisanal breads, including rye, pumpernickel, wheat, cinnamon raisin, and wine breads, among many others. In fact, Orwasher's serves more than 100 types of bread, all made with local ingredients and with no preservatives or enhancers. All of the bread is handmade downstairs in the cellar, which is a fully equipped bread factory with an original brick oven.

Its namesake, Abraham Orwasher, founded the bakery in 1916. His breads were known as some of the best in the city. At one point, his bakery grew to be so popular that he had a very successful wholesale business delivering breads throughout the city with a horse-and-buggy. Eventually, his son, Louis, took over, and then Louis's son sold the bakery to Keith Cohen in 2007. Cohen was intent on keeping things the same while introducing a new era of breads to the neighborhood.

"When I first took over, there were many, many loyal customers that had been purchasing breads here for 20, 30, 40 years," said Cohen. "When they saw my face instead of the previous owner, they wanted to know what I was going to do to the place. It took me a good two years to develop that trust with the old customer base. At the same time, a lot of the new products we've created here have attracted a whole new customer base."

As anyone who has tried it knows, bread making is not child's play. It is an exacting art with demands that can change wildly even with a slight change in weather. All bread begins with a "starter." A starter is a natural form of fermentation—mostly flour and water that has been allowed to sit for a certain amount of time to capture the natural yeast in the air and begin to ferment. With one of Orwasher's breads, customers can literally taste old New York; the bakery still uses a rye starter that has been continuously regenerated since the store opened. Because different kinds of yeast bacteria are indigenous to different areas of the country, they can be used to create different flavors. According to Cohen, a sourdough bread made in San Francisco can have a different taste than one made in New York City because of the different varieties of yeast in the two regions.

As Cohen continues to perfect his breads, he is now offering other local artisanal products as well, like chocolates from a small chocolatier in Brooklyn, local honey, and cheeses. Cohen thinks these items go great with his breads, but it is also a way for him to support other local manufacturers. Orwasher's bread is now in other retail and restaurant establishments, too, including Zabar's, Dean and Deluca, and the Gourmet Garage.

All of this seems to suit the customers just fine. "I had my fair share of naysayers because I was this young kid taking over this historic bakery," said Cohen. "One of the customers called me outside, and I figured 'Uh-oh, I'm going to get a good lashing.' But I have to tell you, she was so complimentary. She really understood what I was trying to do here, and now she's one of my best customers."

ORWASHER'S BAKERY

Established in 1916

308 East 78th Street
Upper East Side, Manhattan
www.orwasherbakery.com
212-288-6569
Subway: 6 train to 77th Street
Open Monday–Saturday:
7:30 a.m. to 7:00 p.m.
Sunday: 9:00 a.m. to 4:00 p.m.

PATSY'S PIZZERIA

Established in 1933

2287-91 First Avenue
East Harlem, Manhattan
www.thepatsyspizza.com 212-534-9783
Subway: 4 or 6 train to 116th Street
Open Monday–Thursday:
11:00 a.m. to 11:00 p.m.
Friday–Saturday: 11:00 a.m. to 12:00 a.m.
Sunday: 11:00 a.m. to 11:00 p.m.

It was one of the very first pizzerias in America, hallowed ground for anyone who loves a slice. Incredibly, Patsy's Pizzeria has been at the same location way up in East Harlem for more than 75 years, proving that when you do something right, people will come find you. "We have people that will fly into LaGuardia, and this is their first stop. We have to put their suitcases in the back while they eat. I mean, this doesn't happen in too many places," said co-owner John Brecevich.

Patsy's was opened in 1933 by Italian immigrant newlyweds Patsy and Carmella Lancieri. The Lancieris were so dedicated to the place they even lived in an apartment above the restaurant. In fact, if one of them was upstairs when the restaurant got busy or a special guest came in, the other would bang on the pipes to call them down. The couple was well-known throughout the neighborhood, with Patsy's becoming a de facto family dining room of sorts—the very essence of an Italian restaurant.

Current owners John Brecevich and Frank Brija took over about 20 years ago and have changed Patsy's very little. The interior has a basic, simple feel to it. Its narrow dining areas are neatly packed with small tables and chairs. Walls are lined with photos of past patrons, both famous and otherwise.

Like any great Italian restaurant, it is the food that takes center stage—classic Northern Italian fare that includes portobello ravioli, gnocchi alla marinara o bolognese, and gamberetti allo scampi. Despite all of the delicious entrees, though, the star of Patsy's will always be the pizza. You won't find any pineapple, buffalo chicken, or any other flavor-of-the-month on these pies. Patsy's just uses classic ingredients. "Simple is always the best," said Brija. "Like our sauce. We haven't changed it probably in 75 years, not even a drop of water, not even a drop of sugar." In fact, Patsy's is so dedicated to maintaining the taste of its sauce that it only buys tomatoes from one grower, who gives the restaurant an exclusive pick of the crop. And, of course, the pizzas have that New York–style thin crust. Patsy's takes it to an extreme, pounding the dough out until it is wafer-thin so the flavor has nowhere to hide. It even uses the same dough machine from when the restaurant first opened.

But it is the coal-fired oven that really sets Patsy's apart. Coal-fired ovens are actually a rarity in New York City because they are now banned. Only establishments that

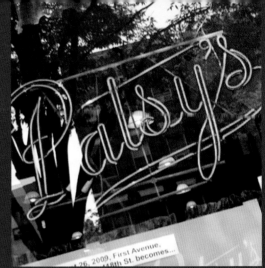

A. 26, 2009, First Avenue, 48th St. becomes...

had coal-fired ovens before the law changed may cook with them, and only a handful survive. The one at Patsy's is the original oven from the 1930s, well seasoned after all these decades. "We have a special oven, 1,000 degrees, and we cook the pizza in no time," said Brecevich. "The pizza has that rustic, honest feel and taste to it." In fact, to help keep the oven consistent, it has never been turned off. Even when Patsy's is closed on Christmas Day, someone comes in to keep the oven fired up.

The delicious food is the main reason Patsy's has such a repeat clientele; both everyday folks and the well-known keep coming back for more. The back dining room area was often a hangout for politicians and movie stars. In fact, a lot of the early organizational meetings for Fiorello LaGuardia mayoral campaigns took place there. It was also an after-hours hot spot for many Broadway performers and jazz musicians. Notable customers include Dean Martin, Rodney Dangerfield, and Frank Sinatra.

Sinatra was not only the biggest star to grace Patsy's, but also its biggest fan. "He used to call Carmella and say, 'I want my friends to experience your pizza, send me 50 pies. Please, whatever it is, I'll pay for it,'" said Brecevich. "And we used to send him the pies and he would serve all his friends and say, 'This is what pizza's supposed to taste like.'"

If that isn't enough of an endorsement from Old Blue Eyes, Brecevich even has an audio recording of him performing at a concert in 1976 and talking about the restaurant. "You ever have pizza at Patsy's at 117th Street?" said Sinatra, prompting the audience to erupt into applause. "Greatest in the world. There ain't nothing like that. I don't care where the hell you go. Even in Italy, you'll never get anything like it." That recording was even used as evidence during a recent court case. The name Patsy's has become so synonymous with great Italian food that there was a lawsuit over the name's use with another Patsy's Restaurant. The Sinatra recording was played to help prove Patsy's status as a legendary pizzeria. "You know, we won in court," said Brecevich. "The court decided that we were the original users of the name Patsy's, so we're entitled to all the rights of the senior user. And we're very proud of that. We feel good about it."

As more people around the world discover this off-the-beaten-path pizzeria, one thing still stays the same. "We figured that simple was always better," said Brija. "If it worked in those days, it still works today, so that's how we stay."

A metal foundry is not something one would expect to find in the heart of Greenwich Village, but instead of churning away in some mundane industrial district on the outskirts of the city, P. E. Guerin sits on Jane Street, a bucolic, semi-residential neighborhood lined with trees and brownstones.

P. E. Guerin is one of the preeminent decorative hardware firms in the country—if not the world—manufacturing doorknobs, hinges, cabinet knobs, and faucets of all shapes and sizes. It creates what many call "jewelry for the home"—the kinds of intricate golden faucets and doorknobs one would expect to find in a room at the Plaza Hotel, the Palace of Versailles, or perhaps Madonna's mansion.

P. E. Guerin has worked out of the same row of unassuming whitewashed brick buildings since 1892. The front door opens into the company's original Victorian showroom, where customers will be greeted by the in-house cats—Pierre, Claude, and Marie Antoinette. Ornate wood cabinets more than 100 years old are filled to the brim with decorative hardware ready for inspection. Above the showroom are three floors of shop rooms, where craftspersons work with tools and in surroundings that have changed very little over the decades. One can easily imagine craftpersons at the same workbenches in the 19th century. And all for good reason, for the techniques and materials P. E. Guerin uses to create its products have stood the test of time.

Like so many other homegrown businesses in New York City, P. E. Guerin's story is an immigrant's tale. Its founder and namesake, Pierre Emmanuel Guerin, immigrated to New York City from Brittany, France, and opened his shop in 1857. After several moves around Lower Manhattan, the business settled at its current location. Amazingly, the company is still owned by the original family. It was passed on to Pierre's son, Emmanuel Pierre Guerin, followed by his son's wife, Marguerita Ward, and then her nephew, Arthur C. Ward. Four generations later, the company is now run by the original owner's great-grandnephew, Andrew F. Ward. And it is not only a tradition for the family, but also for the employees: many of the company's craftspersons have worked here for decades.

One of the most fascinating things about P. E. Guerin is its ordering process. It is probably one of the only places in the country where a client can thumb through any of the company's original catalogs—even those dating back to the 19th century—pick something out, and have it specially made. It is like ordering a custom-made antique. Styles vary from traditional to modern, Art Nouveau to 18th-century French. Hardware can be made in any style, any form. Clients can even create their own designs and P. E. Guerin will bring them to life. Vice President Martin Grubman said clients are often surprised that this much attention to detail is given to just one item, and they often ask if the company requires a minimum order. He enjoys teasing them. "Well, you have to order at least one," he tells them. "We used to do less than one, but it wasn't profitable anymore so we stopped doing that."

The process of making a P. E. Guerin piece has not changed in more than 100 years. Once a client has picked out an item, the original hardware is found in the archive and a mold is created out of sand. The mold is then baked for several hours. A crucible filled with various metals used to make the brass is put into a blast furnace and heated to an incredible 2,000 degrees. The furnace gets so hot that flames scorch out a green hue. Once the brass is properly melted, a three-person team lifts the crucible out of the furnace and carefully—almost delicately—pours the glowing red-orange molten metal into the mold. Watching the pour firsthand, even from 20 feet away, one can feel the waves of intense heat radiating from the molten metal.

P. E. GUERIN

Established in 1857

23 Jane Street, Greenwich Village, Manhattan
www.peguerin.com 212-243-5270
Subway: 1, 2, or 3 train to 14th Street
Open Monday–Friday:
9:00 a.m. to 5:00 p.m.
Call to make an appointment.

LOUIS·XIV
KNOBS

Several minutes after the pour, the mold is ready to be broken and the castings are revealed. The pieces are given an initial brushing to remove excess sand, and then are taken to the plating department, where they are dipped in acid to remove the scale from the surface. Next, they are passed to a filer, who cleans and hand files the surfaces. Then, each piece is taken to a "chaser." Much of the detail is lost during the filing process, so a chaser is a craftsperson who, with little hammers and chisels, re-delineates the piece's design. It is here that P. E. Guerin's artistry sets it apart. The chasers are able to do exquisite handwork that is practically a lost art—moving, shaping, contouring, almost sculpting the metal in ways impossible to do with just casting alone. A chaser can create ornate veins in a decorative vine motif so delicately carved the veins almost look transparent. When finished, the piece is polished, returned to the chaser for another round of detail work, then polished one more time. Last, the surface is prepared, plated, and then a patina is added. Only then is it ready for the ages.

World-renowned decorators and architects—as well as average Joes—regularly visit P. E. Guerin's showroom and have a field day exploring hundreds of floor-to-ceiling drawers, boxes, and cabinets filled with thousands of items created throughout P. E. Guerin's 155-year history. P. E. Guerin has made decorative hardware for some of the most iconic buildings and people in the world, including Henry Ford, the Waldorf-Astoria Hotel, and just about every building designed by famed architects McKim, Meade, and White. It has even made window and door fixtures for Packard automobiles. According to Grubman, P. E. Guerin continues to attract a worldwide clientele because it is one of the only businesses still doing this kind of intricate, labor-intensive, and high-quality work.

Surprisingly, some of these pieces are quite affordable. Stock materials like doorknobs start at $70, while high-end fixtures can go for $600 or more. The Home Depot may be cheaper, but a P. E. Guerin piece is something that was not mass-produced, will never need to be replaced, and will even appreciate in value. Grubman believes that the amount of work P. E. Guerin puts into something simple like a doorknob or faucet is justified when you think of the context in which it is used. "It is the kind of thing that is tactile, that you touch every day, you look at every day," he said. "It is the faucet you turn on when you brush your teeth, the doorknob that you turn daily, the thing that makes you smile every time you touch it. So why wouldn't you want the best?"

There is no shortage of Irish bars in New York City, but unfortunately, they are mostly cookie cutter concoctions thought up by corporate conglomerates. But fear not. There are a few real ones left in the city, ready and waiting to treat their customers like long-lost relatives. One such place is Peter McManus Café.

Located in Chelsea, Peter McManus is the quintessential New York Irish bar and the oldest family-owned bar in the city. It is a relic of old New York that refuses to change, even as the neighborhood continues its conversion into a trendy enclave. Literally a corner bar, it is named after the first owner—Peter McManus— who originally opened the bar across the street in 1911, and then moved to its current location in 1936. McManus would no doubt be thrilled to know that his grandson, James McManus Jr., and his great-grandson, Justin McManus, are now running the place together.

"A lot of bars are popping up now that are trying to be nostalgic places that have that old-time feel, but you just can't create that type of charm. It's something that develops over the ages," said Justin McManus. With its simple food, friendly ambiance, and old-time regulars that have been coming in for 30 years, Peter McManus is a no-frills place that has really become part of the neighborhood. "It's run by a family, not by a consortium," said Jef Klein, historian and author of *The History and Stories of the Best Bars in New York*. "It's not made to look like an Irish bar. It is an Irish bar."

"Someone once said that everything in here is perfectly off balance—whether it's the bright yellow lighting, how every picture on the wall seems to be just a little bit off-center, how there's dips and turns and divots, but it's one of those things where it just shows the wear and tear over the years and how it's still held together," said Justin McManus.

Grand emcee and host of the bar is James McManus Jr., better known to everyone as Jamo and called "the friendliest guy in Manhattan" by Klein. James McManus Sr.—Jamo's father and Justin's grandfather—was thought of as the quintessential Irish bartender during his time. He was such a fixture in the neighborhood that the late comedian Chris Farley once immortalized him as a bartender in a *Saturday Night Live* skit. When James Sr. passed away in 2001, there was a half-page obituary devoted to him in *The New York Times*.

The bar's pride and joy is its original Tiffany stained-glass windows, which grace the back bar and front windows. They are some of the last pieces of Tiffany glass on display in a commercial space in New York City. The glass itself was involved in some drama at the bar some years back. One night, someone actually had the nerve to try and rob James Sr. while he was tending bar. When he refused to give up any money, the robber got off a shot, fortunately hitting the glass and not any people. James Sr., with his military background and all, jumped the bar, tackled the robber outside, and dragged him to the local police precinct. To this day, you can still see the bullet hole in the glass.

The bar itself has been immortalized in a few movies. *Highlander* and Woody Allen's *Radio Days* both shot scenes here. Not all of the bar's brushes with fame were pleasant, though. James Sr. once had to kick out a young actor named Burt Reynolds. Apparently, Reynolds was expressing a negative opinion about the Vietnam War and it did not sit well with the crowd, which at the time was full of longshoremen.

Although the bar's clientele has varied over the years, the customers at Peter McManus are extremely loyal. That loyalty is reciprocated year after year by the McManus family's unfettered hospitality and friendship. "This is a poor man's country club. It's their place; we just run it for them," said Jamo McManus. "You get a thrill, a natural high out of it. It's a great feeling to see people smiling and knowing that you made them enjoy themselves."

PETER MCMANUS CAFÉ

Established in 1936

152 Seventh Avenue
Chelsea, Manhattan
www.facebook.com/pages/
Peter-McManus-Cafe/319879212077
212-929-9691
Subway: 1 or 2 train to 18th Street
Open Monday–Saturday:
10:00 a.m. to 4:00 a.m.
Sunday: 12:00 p.m. to 4:00 a.m.

See Restaurant-Liq[uor]

SAN
KE[?]

Peter McManus and Sons
Tavernmen for Many Years

•

When you hear the name Peter McManus mentioned, it is
a name synonomous with the tavern industry, dating way back
[...] arrived in this country in 1906, and he and his
[...] tavern on Second

A "New
conducted by
[...] Manhattan

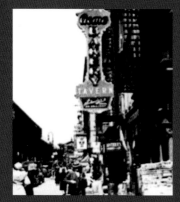

P. J. CLARKE'S

Established in 1884

915 Third Avenue
Upper East Side, Manhattan
www.pjclarkes.com 212-317-1616
Subway: E or M train
to Lexington Avenue–53rd Street
Open daily 11:30 a.m. to 4:00 a.m.

It is one of the oldest restaurants in America and quite possibly one of the friendliest, for its doors have welcomed everyone from yesterday's longshoremen to today's hipsters. Just looking at P. J. Clarke's on the Manhattan landscape, you'll know you are onto something special, for its modest 19th-century building pokes through a cavernous valley of skyscrapers. It is an old-world holdout standing defiantly against its modern surroundings.

As longtime customer Tom Hill put it, "The ambiance is kind of what you would expect and want it to be. It's got a wonderful old but comfortable and classic sort of feeling, and it feels genuine, not artificially made to look this way. This is real."

The restaurant was built in 1884 and was originally called Shivley's. Around 1890, Patrick Joseph Clarke emigrated from Ireland and started bartending there. Within 10 years, he had saved enough money to buy the restaurant and put his name on the door. Since 1909, P. J. Clarke's has changed ownership just twice. Most of that time the restaurant was in the hands of brothers Joseph and Daniel Lavezzo, who always understood and protected the cultural importance of the place. They proved their dedication in 1967 when there were plans to put up a 47-story skyscraper and demolish the building. Today, the skyscraper is

there, but a deal was worked out to build it around Clarke's.

In 2000, the Lavezzo family decided to sell. The buyers were a group of investors that included former Yankees owner George Steinbrenner and actor Timothy Hutton. Veteran restaurateur Phil Scotti led the group, and he was determined to keep P. J. Clarke's around for another 100 years. When they purchased it, the building desperately needed structural repair. The owners hatched a plan to take out the building's entire contents—including the floors and ceiling—pack them up, and put them in storage for months while reinforced steel, plumbing, and other structural elements were put in. Then, working with detailed photographs, they put everything back in exactly as it was before. The restoration was so unobtrusive that several longtime patrons actually complained—they could not see what the new owners had done to the place and wondered why it took so long to reopen.

Even after the restoration, the restaurant's interior has changed very little. Looking much like it did in the 19th century, it is a classic tavern space—from the tiny tiles on the floor to the wood-paneled walls, from the old boxing photos on the wall to the stuffed dog on the shelf. If there is any question as to whether or not this is an authentic Irish bar, look no further than the ceiling. There, poking out of the woodwork, are two human leg bones, rumored to be an Irish good luck charm. As for the stuffed dog, it was apparently a stray named Skippy who started hanging around the bar in the late 1930s, becoming its unofficial mascot. Unfortunately, the dog met a sad demise when it was hit by an automobile in front of the bar. A collection was taken and the dog was sent to the taxidermist so it could be immortalized on the shelf.

And what about the food? Let's just say if something's not broke, don't fix it.

"The food here is honest. Everything is delivered fresh every day. We have a freezer that is about the size of a regular home freezer, and the only thing we keep in it is ice cream," said a former manager.

P. J. Clarke's is known for classic American food like chicken potpie, prime steaks, roasted cod, and macaroni and cheese. Its burgers are particularly fawned over. As the story goes, singer Nat King Cole once bit into the bacon cheeseburger and exclaimed, "The Cadillac of burgers!" Today, regular patrons tell the wait staff, "Gimme a Cadillac."

Nat King Cole is not the only celebrity who loved P. J. Clarke's; Marilyn Monroe, Louis Armstrong, and Joan Crawford have all dined here as well. Jacqueline Kennedy Onassis supposedly loved the restaurant's spinach salads. Musician Buddy Holly even proposed to his wife, Maria, here. But perhaps the biggest name to dine on P. J. Clarke's red-checkered tablecloths was Old Blue Eyes himself, Frank Sinatra. He even owes the restaurant a bit of gratitude, and not just for its delicious burgers. One of his greatest hits—"One For My Baby" by Johnny Mercer—was actually written at the bar.

The story goes that Mercer was sitting at the bar by himself at three o'clock in the morning and that he had lost his woman. The bartender was about to close and Mercer was writing the lyrics out on a napkin at the bar. In the song, the bartender's name is Joe, but the actual bartender was Tommy Joyce. As the lyrics go, "It's quarter to three, there's no one in the place except you and me. So set 'em up Joe, I got a little story." Mercer later called the bartender to apologize, telling him he just couldn't get his name to rhyme.

"One For My Baby" is not the restaurant's only claim to fame; it was also featured in the 1945 film *The Lost Weekend*, starring Ray Milland and directed by Billy Wilder. Due to the cramped quarters and noisy elevated trains outside, only one scene was shot in P. J. Clarke's. Today, filmmakers would have plenty of space to shoot, for P. J. Clarke's has opened up two more locations in Manhattan—one downtown and another at Lincoln Center. The restaurant has also expanded to Washington, D.C., Las Vegas, and even Sao Paulo, Brazil.

As P. J. Clarke's expands, one thing remains the same: the loyalty of its customers. And there's one customer who will be around forever—former Saint Louis Cardinals infielder Phil Kennedy. He used to come here in the afternoons and hold court with boxers Rocky Graziano and Jake Lamotta and singer Alice Faye, among others. In fact, he spent so much time at P. J. Clarke's that his wife requested that his ashes be placed in the restaurant after his death, as he spent more time there than with her. Since 1985, there has been a small wooden box next to the bottles behind the bar.

It is not just the food and ambiance that keeps regulars coming back to P. J. Clarke's. It's dedication. "There's a different type of expectation when you walk into this restaurant. All these Upper Eastside customers eating hamburgers with their hands—they feel like they're doing their part to make P. J. Clarke's what it is. They're doing their part to uphold an institution," said a former manager.

There was a time when SoHo was actually an industrial area devoid of any art galleries or fashion models. It was a place where craftsmen plied their trades, making goods that were sold worldwide. That era is gone now, but there are still remnants of it tucked between the high-end boutiques that line the streets of the neighborhood.

The Putnam Rolling Ladder Company is a perfect example. Ladders are its trade—extension ladders, straight ladders, step stools, just about any kind—but its specialty is rolling ladders, ones used in spaces like libraries and old stockrooms. It is one of only a handful of companies in the world still making these kinds of ladders.

The classic Rolling Ladder No. 1 is the standard that has defined the company, a design that has not changed since the business opened in 1905. "It will last longer than your house; it will last longer than your life," said company president Gregg Monsees. "We sell them to stores in New York and then we buy them back when the stores go out of business." Brooks Brothers, Coach, Bell Telephone, and Foot Locker are just a few of the company's clients.

PUTNAM ROLLING LADDER COMPANY

Established in 1905

32 Howard Street, SoHo, Manhattan
www.putnamrollingladder.com
212-226-5147
Subway: N, R, Q, J, Z, or 6 train
to Canal Street
Open Monday–Friday:
8:00 a.m. to 4:00 p.m.

These days, many use Putnam rolling ladders in their homes as decorative pieces in libraries, wine cellars, or lofts. Each rolling ladder is custom-made; they come in just about any type of wood imaginable and can be up to 14 feet tall. Everyone from John Lennon to former President George W. Bush has one, and Putnam has shipped as far away as New Zealand. Once, an Alaskan fisherman even offered to barter freshly caught salmon for a ladder.

The business was started by Samuel Putnam in 1905 and has been owned by just two families. The Monsees family bought the business in 1946, and a few years later Gregg Monsees's father, Warren, became president. He remained president and worked full time at the company until his death in 2009 at age 87. He would even regularly make the trek out to the factory in Bushwick, Brooklyn, where many of the components are made. All of the components are handmade using almost the same tools and techniques as when the business first opened.

When orders come in, the side rails are chosen from the company's supply of lumber and cut to the correct length. Then, an employee adds grooves to the sides of the rails. To create the steps, a special machine is used to drill two holes into the edges at the same time. The steps are then sanded and smoothed. During assembly, the ladders are stained, hardware is added, and, if necessary, the ladder tracks for rolling ladders are bent at 90-degree angles using a special machine. Finally, the ladders are packed and shipped to an eagerly awaiting customer.

Visiting the company's offices is a treat in itself, for the place is literally a time capsule. Housed in an old cast-iron building dating back to 1886, its exterior is designated a historic New York landmark. Inside, the old workshop has a beautiful tin ceiling. The tools and machinery look like antiques, but are used daily. The wooden Putnam and Company sign above the main entrance is more than 100 years old and was originally on the side of a horse-and-buggy that was used to deliver ladders to customers. It is now one of the oldest advertisement signs still in use in New York City.

Luckily, Putnam bought this beautiful building and the one next door in the 1940s. According to Monsees, due to the high real estate prices in the neighborhood, the buildings are now worth more than the business. Putnam has had numerous offers to sell, but its desire to preserve the company is too strong. "We're an institution in the United States and in New York," said Monsees. "We own the building and we're secure. We're not leaving."

RUSS & DAUGHTERS

Established in 1914

179 East Houston Street
Lower East Side, Manhattan
www.russanddaughters.com
212-475-4880
Subway: F train to 2nd Avenue
Open Monday–Friday: 8:00 a.m. to 8:00 p.m.
Saturday: 9:00 a.m. to 7:00 p.m.
Sunday: 8:00 a.m. to 5:30 p.m.

Few people have ever heard of an appetizing store, which is a bit surprising considering at one time they were almost as common as the corner deli in New York City. Now only a few survive. Luckily, Russ & Daughters is one of them—a wonderful example of an old-world business working surprisingly well in the modern world.

The Russ & Daughters storefront looks a bit out of place these days on Houston Street. It is one of the last vestiges of the Lower East Side when the Lower East Side was, well, the Lower East Side—a bustling ghetto full of recent immigrants trying to get a foothold in America. And it was to these immigrants—particularly Eastern European Jews—that Russ & Daughters first catered.

Appetizing is a sister food tradition to delicatessen. It stems from Jewish dietary laws, which prohibit meat and dairy from being eaten or purchased together. A delicatessen is where customers go for meat products and an appetizing store is where they go for fish and dairy products. "Simply put, an appetizing store is the place you go to get anything you would possibly want to put on a bagel: smoked salmon, cream cheeses, spreads, or herring," explained fourth-generation co-owner Niki Russ Federman.

Although the store sells many different items—including homemade salads, spreads, and a wide variety of sweet treats like babka and rugelach—Russ & Daughters is particularly well-known for its variety of smoked fish, including sturgeon, sable, whitefish, chubs, tuna, and 10 varieties of smoked salmon.

"Smoked salmon is actually like wine," said fourth-generation co-owner Josh Russ Tupper. "You come into Russ & Daughters, and you can taste 10 different kinds. Each one is going to have its own unique flavor palette and texture and its own story, depending upon how it has been smoked, where it came from, and the season."

Russ & Daughters has been at this location on Houston Street since the 1920s. The shop began like many Lower East Side businesses: with a pushcart. "My great-grandfather Joel Russ started the business in 1908," said Federman. "He had a pushcart right around the corner, on Orchard Street, from which he sold herring and pickled lox and Polish mushrooms. In 1914, my great-grandfather scraped together enough money to open up his store. It was originally around the corner and then, in 1920, he opened this current location and we've been here ever since."

Joel Russ was quite the innovator, even if it was due to circumstance rather than choice. He had no sons but three daughters—Hattie, Anne, and Ida—who worked with him in the store. Federman claimed it was the first business in the country to recognize women's participation within the name of the business. Initially, the name "Russ & Daughters" caused quite a stir. People would stop their delivery trucks on the street, perplexed if not somewhat offended by someone who would name his business after his daughters. "I'd like to think that my great-grandfather was a pioneering feminist," said Federman, smiling. "But I think, honestly, if he had had sons, it would've been Russ & Sons."

His daughters actually turned out to be an asset, though. Joel Russ didn't really understand the concept of customer service, but having his charming and affable daughters working behind the counter really helped to soften the feel of the store. The daughters even met their husbands through the store, with all three men eventually coming to work with the family.

People still come to Russ & Daughters as much to be in the store as they do for the food. In addition to the excellent customer service, which has lasted through the ages, there is a special energy here. When a customer walks into Russ & Daughters, they are connected to a living 100-year-old tradition. Niki Russ Federman and her cousin, Josh Russ Tupper, are currently running things together, along with a staff that includes some employees who have been working at the store for decades. General Manager Herman Vargas has been working behind the counter since he was a teenager.

"Nothing can compare to food that is prepared with 100-year-old traditions," said Federman. "Some of these recipes go back to my great-grandfather's time and we have upheld the quality, the artisanal production, of these foods." The smoked salmon is sliced by hand; nothing in a package from a supermarket could ever compare, either in terms of quality and freshness of the fish or in the artistry of how it is prepared. Even the bagels at Russ & Daughters are more authentic. They are smaller and have a firmer crust so customers can really taste the toppings or fillings rather than just the bread.

The store continues to be a family-run business. And now that the next generation of Russ & Daughters is firmly in place, they understand this is about more than just carrying on a family name. "It took me a long time to realize that being a part of this legacy was actually a gift," said Federman. "I was at a party once and the musician Lou Reed happened to be there. I had brought some smoked salmon, of course, and he was loving it. He introduced himself to me and said, 'I really wanted to meet you. You're New York royalty.' My jaw dropped, and I thought, 'Lou Reed? No, you're New York royalty.' Of course, I'm not royalty, but it made me see how important this place is to so many people and my responsibility to keep its traditions going."

There is a place on the Lower East Side where everybody can—at least for the evening—feel a little bit Jewish. Just walking into the place is like crashing a bar mitzvah. It is Sammy's Roumanian Steak House, a place where old meets new and traditional meets eclectic. For whatever reason, this mix works wonderfully.

Sammy's sits in a section of the Lower East Side on Chrystie Street, which was once the epicenter of early Jewish-American culture. It is one of the last holdouts from that bygone era. It is kind of hard to describe the restaurant. First, there is the interior that looks straight out of a men's lodge basement—complete with its drop ceiling, cluttered but clean dining space, and kitschy decor. Then, there are the old-world touches like seltzer and genuine schmaltz at every table, a lounge singer in the front, and, of course, homestyle cooking and staff members who treat customers like extended family.

To the uninitiated, Sammy's may look like it is from another era, if not another world. It's certainly an acquired taste. "You either get it or you don't get it," said owner David Zimmerman. "Most people get it, thank God. That's why we've always been here. But, you know, we're on the Lower East Side, and it's very old-school New York. It's not the Four Seasons. It's not fancy." Even so, once customers spend some time at the restaurant—listening to the music, eating the pickles or chopped liver, and drinking the frozen vodka—they suddenly "get it."

The history of Sammy's is a classic New York tale. It has been around for about 80 years, known for a time as the Parkway, a Jewish steakhouse. The Zimmerman family has owned the place since 1975, when Zimmerman's father, Stanley, won the restaurant in a poker game. Many of the staff members have been with Zimmerman since the 1970s. As for the name of the restaurant—Sammy's Roumanian Steak House—it often leads to confusion. "Funny, nobody here is Romanian, nobody speaks Romanian,

nobody is from Romania," said Zimmerman. "We just left the sign when we took over. But it fits this place."

According to Zimmerman, it was his father, Stanley, who really gave the restaurant its schtick, including the vodka bottles frozen in blocks of ice, the nonstop entertainment, and the sing-alongs and dancing. Then there are the walls, which are covered with literally thousands of photographs of customers and their families, part of a tradition at Sammy's. "We call the walls Jewish wallpaper," said Zimmerman.

But don't let the kitschy decor and traditions fool you. This place has some serious accolades when it comes to food. *The New York Times* gave it three stars and *Condé Nast* calls it one of the top 50 restaurants in America. Its specialty is Jewish-style cuisine with an Eastern-European bent. All the standards are here: kishka, chopped liver, sweet breads, potato pancakes, and—of course—sour pickles at every table. The star is the Romanian skirt steak, seasoned with kosher salt and smeared with garlic. "We serve it by the pound—one pound is a small, two pounds is a medium, and three pounds is a large. I usually tell people it goes by shirt size," said Zimmerman. To wash it all down, customers can try another New York classic—egg creams. And customers need not worry about their stomachs—Sammy's offers free Alka-Seltzer at the door.

While at Sammy's, don't be shocked if you end up sitting next to a bigwig CEO or celebrity, for they too appreciate Sammy's stripped-down and relaxed setting, which is reminiscent of Sunday dinner at Grandma's. Matthew Broderick, Billy Crystal, and Eli Manning have all dined here.

As people make the trek to this little restaurant in a basement on the Lower East Side, they can be assured that change is not in the cards here. "I will never change the decor. Half my family's pictures are on the wall, plus all of our customers and their families. I can't take that away from them. This is their place," said Zimmermann.

SAMMY'S ROUMANIAN STEAK HOUSE

Established in 1975

157 Chrystie Street
Lower East Side, Manhattan
212-673-0330
Subway: D train to Grand Street
Open Sunday–Thursday:
4:00 p.m. to 9:30 p.m.
Friday–Saturday: 4:00 p.m. to 11:00 p.m.

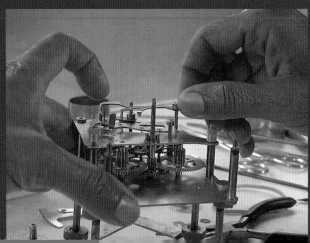

SUTTON CLOCK SHOP

Established in 1966

139 East 61st Street, Upper East Side, Manhattan
www.suttonclocks.com 212-758-2260
Subway: 4, 5, 6, N, Q, or R train
to Lexington Avenue–59th Street
Open Tuesday–Friday: 11:00 a.m. to 4:00 p.m.

It is comforting to know that a repair shop like Sutton Clock Shop prospers in New York City. We live in a throwaway culture, where new is often thought of as better, but for many people, a clock that has been in their home or business for years or even decades becomes a part of their family. "There is a sentimental value that cannot be replaced. Clocks often remind you of a place, a certain part of your life, and you want to hang onto that. It's kind of like a photograph," said Sebastian Laws, owner and purveyor of Sutton Clock Shop.

Sebastian Laws's father, Knud Christiansen, started the shop about 60 years ago. An emigrant from Denmark, he was a rower for his country's 1936 Olympic rowing team. Now in his 90s, and still healthy and alert, Christiansen stops in on occasion to check on things and help his son with the latest clock challenge.

The shop is located on the second floor of a building on the corner of Lexington and 61st Street. When approaching the building, one can actually see Laws perched at his worktable by the window from the street. Inside Laws's tiny shop are hundreds of clocks of every imaginable shape and design, taking up every inch of available space. Some are for sale; others are just here for repair. Laws's mechanical patients range from barometers and clocks dating back to the 18th century to the plastic cartoon-character clocks of today. Customers are welcome to drop off their clocks during the day; often Laws can give a free estimate right on the spot. Turnaround time for repair is usually two weeks.

House calls are not uncommon. Laws will work on anything from a pocket watch to enormous bank clocks or grandfather clocks that are too big to take into the shop. He won't fix cuckoo clocks though; they are often too cheaply made to repair and are not worth the headache.

According to Laws, the learning process never ends, especially with the older clocks. "A lot of the older ones were made by individual clock makers. Every little town had its own clock maker, and it would always try to do something unique. So when you open up these clocks, each one is a little different. You sort of have to get into the mindset of the clock maker who was building it," he said. There is a bright side to these old clocks, though. Many times clocks that are more than 150 years old work better than newly made ones. Laws will often repair antique parts rather than install new ones because the quality just isn't as good.

When it comes to clock repair, slow and simple is best. "I just tend to like the old-school way of doing it," said Laws. "For me, it's sort of peaceful; it's like you're one with the clock. Sometimes there will be a problem that I can't figure out at first. I like to sort of contemplate and sleep on it and come back the next day. Usually, I then realize what's wrong with the clock."

One of the most important things Laws has learned while running his shop is that the true value of a clock is determined by its owner. "I don't look at a clock in terms of value or quality, but rather in terms of what it means to people," he said. "Someone will bring in a really bad clock, like a wind-up chicken eating a worm or something like that, and be really enthusiastic about it. That gets me excited and makes me want to work on it."

TINY DOLL HOUSE

Established in 1984

314 East 78th Street, Upper East Side, Manhattan
www.tinydollhouse.co 212-744-3719
Subway: 6 train to 77th Street
Open Monday–Saturday: 11:00 a.m. to 5:00 p.m.
Closed Sunday

You might be surprised to hear that New York City has quite the dollhouse enthusiast culture, but it's true. Countless locals love designing and furnishing exquisite Lilliputian households and objects. If you think about it, it makes quite a bit of sense, for New Yorkers are severely limited in terms of living space. "I think a lot of the fascination has to do with enabling customers to create a home that they may never have—a cottage in the country, a Victorian house by the sea, a Georgian townhouse. It gives people the opportunity to create another environment and to fantasize about living in that environment," said owner Leslie Edelman.

For about 25 years now, Tiny Doll House has been helping New Yorkers deck out these miniature dream houses, which are often furnished better than the collector's own homes. Many times they include miniature versions of furnishings New York apartment dwellers can only dream about: china hutches, dining room tables, and (gasp!) even backyards. A Home Depot for doll culture, Tiny Doll House has everything from hand-printed wallpaper and shag carpet to ceramic tiles and tiny bricks. The details are astounding—hand-laid parquet floors, turned spindles for staircases, and milled crown molding.

If an object can be found in a real home, Tiny Doll House most likely has a miniaturized version of it. There is a full line of furniture in several styles and tastes, full sterling silver sets, and toys for kids. There are miniature pieces of food, such as Chinese takeout and coffee in Starbucks cups. And for the tech-savvy doll enthusiast, there are flat-screen televisions and even iPads.

Dollhouses start at just a couple hundred dollars, but for the well-heeled doll there are custom-built townhouses and brownstones that go for thousands of dollars. It is not unheard of for someone to spend $15,000 on a fully furnished dollhouse. It should come as no surprise, then, that the shop has quite a few celebrity clients. Tiny Doll House's list of notable customers includes Joan Rivers, Kevin Bacon, Rene Russo, and Sigourney Weaver. But that certainly shouldn't scare away a doll enthusiast on a budget; no matter what your skill level or price range, you are welcome at Tiny Doll House. "We cater to all ranges of collectors," said Edelman. "You can buy a chandelier for $9 or you can buy one for $570."

And it's not just little girls and grown women who enjoy dollhouses. There are men who enjoy building houses around specific historical themes, and even little boys who are attracted to the construction aspect of it. Collectors are also big customers. Many of the pieces that Tiny Doll House sells are handmade and signed by artisans known around the world. Often their pieces appreciate in value over the years, becoming an investment.

Tiny Doll House also creates custom houses for clients in its downstairs workshop. Many of these projects are replicas of the customers' own homes or homes from their childhoods. "We have many customers who had a dollhouse when they were young and, for one reason or another, lost it along the way. Now that they're grown, they want to recapture that feeling of being children again," said Edelman.

Shooting a firearm in Manhattan—legally? Believe it or not, just about anyone—even if you've never touched a firearm before—can go to the Westside Rifle and Pistol Range and fire off a few rounds.

Located in the Flatiron District, a place known more for stilettos and designer collections than .45s and shell casings, Westside has a clientele as diverse as a New York subway car. Aside from the obvious law-enforcement types practicing their marksmanship and the occasional actor researching a role, Westside also hosts couples looking for a change from the bar scene, regular folks curious about firing off a gun, and even bridesmaids out for a bachelorette party. "It's funny. It used to be mostly men, but in the last 20 years it has flipped. The majority of our customers now are women bringing their boyfriends here," said instructor John Aaron. The diverse crowd is due in part to Westside's friendly reputation. Staffers are eager to dispel negative myths about guns and their owners while showing newcomers that marksmanship is a fun sport—not to mention a whole lot cheaper than therapy.

A no-frills space painted in light blue, Westside's subterranean shooting gallery has a clubby atmosphere to it, albeit with the smell of gunpowder wafting through the air and muffled bangs coming from the shooting area. Tables and benches facing the shooting gallery are often filled with "regulars" who sometimes stop by just to hang out. Guns and accessories are sold at the in-house gun shop, along with a few cheeky items, like paper zombie targets.

Inside the double-doored shooting gallery is a long bank of shooting desks, each outfitted with its own target lane. A sense of déjà vu may hit first-time visitors; several movies and television shows have been filmed here. The list includes several episodes of *Law and Order* and, most famously, the movie *Taxi Driver*. The pivotal scene in which Robert DeNiro's character takes target practice was filmed here.

Murray Michaels and Jerry Prizant opened Westside Rifle and Pistol Range in 1963. After a few ownership changes over the years, Darren Lee Young took over in 1992 and has been running the place ever since. So why is it located in the Flatiron District? Back in the 1960s, the area was known for its cheap rents and close proximity to a couple of police precincts. Now, even with the neighborhood completely transformed, Westside gels surprisingly well with its surroundings. Locals know it well; if they haven't tried it yet, it is definitely on their to-do list.

Do you think you're ready to fire off a few rounds yourself? All it takes is a valid driver's license and permanent U.S. citizen status. You also have to be at least 21 years old (sorry, no Sweet 16 birthday parties here). First-timers must register online so that Westside can do a criminal background check in advance, which usually takes two days.

On your scheduled shoot day, you—along with the other rookies—are given a classroom demonstration on gun usage and safety. Next, it is off to the table and benches, where everyone is given a box of Winchester bullets and instructed on how to fill the rifle magazine. It is also during this time that the instructor pointedly suggests to anyone thinking of taking a bullet home as a souvenir that it is a bad idea. It's likely that you'll forget it's in your pocket or purse and may have a tough time explaining it to the NYPD later.

Once in the range, everyone gets his or her own booth and target. Most people take to shooting like a duck to water, often pleasantly surprised at how well they hit the target. "What I find is that people are freaked out by what they see of guns and firearms on television, but once they get past the anxiety, they enjoy themselves tremendously. I've never had anyone here who has left disappointed," said Aaron.

WESTSIDE RIFLE AND PISTOL RANGE

Established in 1963

20 West 20th Street
Flatiron District, Manhattan
www.westsidepistolrange.com
212-929-7287
Subway: F, V, N, R, or W train
to 23rd Street; 1 train to 18th Street
Open Monday–Friday:
9:00 a.m. to 9:00 p.m.
Saturday: 9:00 a.m. to 5:00 p.m.
Sunday: 9:00 a.m. to 3:00 p.m.

WORTH AND WORTH

Established in 1922

45 West 57th Street, No. 602
Midtown, Manhattan
www.hatshop.com 212-265-2887
Subway: N, Q, or R train
to Fifth Avenue–59th Street
Open Monday–Tuesday:
10:00 a.m. to 6:00 p.m.
Wednesday–Saturday:
10:00 a.m. to 7:00 p.m.

Sometimes it's good to go backward. That's just what one New York City business did, and in the process it reinvented itself for the 21st century. The shop is Worth and Worth, well-known in the Big Apple for decades as the quintessential hat shop.

Worth and Worth is a shop that you have to search out rather than stumble upon. Though it's on 57th Street, just a stone's throw from Fifth Avenue, it is located on the sixth floor. And that's just the way owner Orlando Palacios likes it. "People feel comfortable perched up here away from the hustle-and-bustle. It's almost like a cozy social club," he said. Along the walls are shelves filled with dozens of hat styles—including fedoras, Panamas, driving caps, stingy brims, bowlers, and even Sherlock Holmes–style hats—all with a certain liveliness and individuality.

In 1999, the company was lumbering. Its then-owner, Harold Rosenholtz, admitted his heart just wasn't in it anymore. That year, Orlando Palacios, one of Rosenholtz's employees, bought the business and did something unthinkable. He completely transformed it—Worth and Worth would no longer just be selling hats, it would be making them, too. Now, with clients all over the world, Palacios has never looked back. "We say what goes in every handmade Worth and Worth hat is blood, sweat, and love. Blood because sometimes we prick our little fingers, sweat because it's a labor-intensive work, and love because it's our trade," he said.

The back room, where many of the hats are created and styled, is called the "kitchen." Palacios's small staff works with vintage hat-making tools and machinery, giving the room the feeling of an old craftsman's shop. "See this one?" he said, pointing to a stout sewing machine from the Victorian age. "I've taken old machines like this and reengineered them to do a specific stitch. So we can do all of this little tweaking that no one else will or can do."

Worth and Worth is one of the oldest haberdasheries in New York. Started in 1922, it began in the lobby of the Astor Hotel in present-day Times Square. Eventually, the business moved to a townhouse on Fifth Avenue and expanded its business to sell pants, suits, and ties as well. Then, in the 1950s, Harvey Kane took over and moved the focus back to hats. Kane's son-in-law, Harold Rosenholtz, took over the day-to-day operations in the 1970s and elevated the shop to its international stature by continually updating the product line and making sure it was advertised in all the right places.

Today, Worth and Worth is the only Manhattan hat shop still creating a men's hat in-house from start to finish. The hats are made of straw, cashmere, beaver, rabbit, or a variety of other materials. There are even felts from Portugal, Italy, and the Czech Republic—all known for their high quality. Among the shop's more exquisite hats are its legendary Montecristi Panamas, which are made in Ecuador by local weavers. The Montecristis are stunning works of art, often taking more than a year to weave. Each hat is a documented, cataloged, and signed piece given the same prestige as expensive jewelry, and many sell for more than $10,000.

Though the Montecristis may be a little over budget for most people, Worth and Worth sells hats for every pocketbook. Clients come from all walks of life—ranging from businesspersons on their lunch break to rock stars looking for a new look. And no project is too small or too big. Whether it's a sequined top hat for an individual client in the Midwest or the actual fedora Michael Jackson wore in his "Smooth Criminal" music video, Worth and Worth is always looking for a challenge.

Movie productions are a constant source of new business. Wardrobe directors are always stopping in for everything from period hats to one-of-a-kind creations. Worth and Worth recently finished a top hat for actor James Franco, who will wear it in the upcoming movie *Oz: The Great and Powerful*, a prequel to *The Wizard of Oz*. "It was basically a turn-of-the-century top hat, but because it's the movies they wanted it taller than normal for more effect," said Palacios.

For decades, formal hats have been on the downslide as everyday wear. Many point to John F. Kennedy's lack of a hat during his inaugural address as the beginning of the end. Hat makers even have an inside joke that it was a hat maker who actually killed Kennedy. But luckily, formal hats are making a comeback. According to Palacios, one of the reasons is Hollywood. "The younger generation of movie actors are wearing them, so you know the general public will follow their idols," he said. He also believes that hats fell out of style during the 1960s because anything associated with conformity was frowned upon. "But now, when you think of something like a classic fedora, what do you think? Granddad. And Granddad was cool. And stylish," he said.

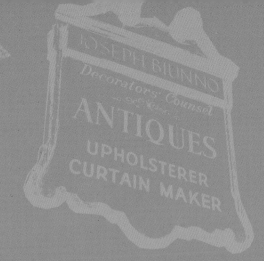

QUEENS

BELLITTE BICYCLES

Established in 1918

169-20 Jamaica Avenue, Jamaica, Queens
www.bellbikes.com 718-739-3795
Subway: F train to 169th Street
Open Monday–Saturday: 10:00 a.m. to 6:00 p.m.
Hours vary during the summer. It is best to call ahead.

New Yorkers have always had a love affair with bicycles. Part of the city's landscape for more than 100 years, bicycles are used for commuting, exercising, or just sightseeing around the Big Apple. One bike shop in Jamaica, Queens, understands this love affair especially well—Bellitte Bicycles. It has been in business since the end of World War I; not only is it the largest bike shop in Queens, it is also the oldest family-owned bike shop in America.

Bellitte's good reputation is well-known. The shop, which incredibly is still in its original spot, has been a mainstay on Jamaica Avenue since 1918, even before the busy thoroughfare was a paved road. Even though it is located in a far eastern section of Queens—almost touching Long Island—New Yorkers come from all over to visit. According to third-generation co-owner Sal Bellitte, the shop has thrived over the years for one main reason—bicycles are products that consumers have learned not to buy from big-box chain stores. Since bikes have a lot of moving parts and get banged up a bit, they need to be serviced every once in a while. To stay in business, places like Bellitte Bicycles shine with their customer service and repairs. From youngsters looking for their first bike to the city's bike messengers coming in for specialty equipment, all are given the same caring service.

The shop has not changed much through the generations. It is a fairly small place in which the latest in bicycle technology coexists with vintage fixtures and signs. The walls are painted in bright red and yellow stripes. There are bicycles stuck in every nook and cranny of the store, including on the ceiling. Lining the walls are old wooden bike racks that once showcased chrome-laden Schwinn bicycles, but now display everything from BMX bicycles to the latest carbon-fiber frame racing models. The shop also carries biking accessories of every imaginable need, from old-fashioned rubber honking horns to giant baskets specially designed for pizza deliveries.

One item at Bellitte is particularly cherished, displayed up in a corner like a grand old dame watching over the place. It is a rare antique Pierce-Arrow bicycle complete with wooden rims. This black beauty was sold to a gentleman in the early 1920s by Sal's grandfather, Sam Bellitte, the founder of the store. Sam and the gentleman quickly became friends, but over time, the man stopped coming in. One day, years later, the gentleman's granddaughter came into the store with the bicycle, and explained that her grandfather had passed away. "One of his dying wishes was for the bicycle to be brought back to his friend who sold it to him," said Bellitte.

Sam Bellitte initially opened the business as a motorcycle, bicycle, and radio shop. It was quite a combination, but he was determined to make it work. One of the family stories passed down over the years was about how

the grand opening wasn't so grand. "He was extremely depressed and he went to his wife and told her he basically sold two batteries for 65 cents," explained Sal Bellitte. "Grandmother told him, 'Don't worry; you're going to make a success out of this.'"

And he did. Soon afterwards, business did pick up. For a time, Bellitte Bicycles was even the largest seller of Indian motorcycles in America. Unfortunately, the Great Depression killed off that side of the business, but it actually helped bicycle sales. New Yorkers were in need of a cheap mode of transportation to get around the city and bicycles easily fit the bill.

It wasn't the Depression, but rather World War II that brought Bellitte Bicycles its toughest years. Bicycle manufacturers were put to work making parts for the war effort, which left little time for their actual product. Bicycles were still being produced, but essential pieces like chains and pedals were absent due to rationing. The Bellittes were industrious, though. They had bikes sent to the shop anyway and then scoured Queens for old bicycle parts to use on the new ones. Thus, they kept the business afloat.

By the time the 1950s rolled in, Bellitte Bicycles was going gangbusters, stocking some 10,000 bicycles at a time, more than any shop of its kind in the world. The best years for Bellitte Bicycles were the 1970s, though. Apparently that pesky oil embargo and subsequent energy shortage encouraged a lot of people to go back to bikes. It truly was the golden era for bicycles, with sales increasing more than any other time.

Today, Bellitte Bicycles still does a robust business. It is now run by Sal Bellitte, his cousin's husband, Peter Frouws, and his sister's husband, Karl Herzer. And the fourth generation has been coming around, too. Bellitte's son Michael and daughter Melissa work at the store on the weekends. And let us not forget Sal's father, Vincent Bellitte, who started working here in 1927. Now in his 90s, he still comes in occasionally to make sure the shop is running smoothly.

It is a good time to be in the bike business. America's recent economic problems and renewed concern about the environment has done nothing but help the world of bicycling, particularly in New York City. Some people are quite surprised to hear how wonderful a place it is to ride a bicycle. Not only are the sights and sounds of the city enough to keep cyclists entertained for hours, but the city has also made great strides to accommodate riders. Every year more and more bike paths and lanes are added to the streets and most parks now have bike-friendly areas. The city also hosts numerous biking events throughout the year.

BOHEMIAN HALL
AND BEER GARDEN

Established in 1910

29-19 24th Avenue, Astoria, Queens
www.bohemianhall.com 718-274-4925
Subway: N or Q train to Astoria-Ditmars
Open Monday–Wednesday: 5:00 p.m. to 3:00 a.m.
Thursday–Friday: 5:00 p.m. to 4:00 a.m.
Saturday: 12:00 p.m. to 4:00 a.m.
Sunday: 12:00 p.m. to 3:00 am.

Walking along 24th Avenue in Astoria, Queens, one cannot help but notice a pair of enormous wooden arched doors leading into a walled-off block. The doors are a gate to a bygone era, a place where old-world Europeans found friendship and community in an unknown land. It is the Bohemian Hall and Beer Garden, one of the first in America and the last of its kind in New York City. It is a much-needed bucolic oasis in this land of concrete and skyscrapers, a place where one can enjoy food and drink along with great company.

The concept of a beer garden developed in southern Germany during the 19th century in cities like Munich. They were basically open-air parcels of land where beer and food were served. A typical beer garden was attached to a beer hall, brewery, or drinking establishment. Beer gardens became popular places for the working class to meet and socialize.

According to Lucy Reynolds, manager of the Bohemian Hall and Beer Garden, the concept has not been lost on today's New Yorkers. "New York City is a place where people work a lot. It's very stressful and they are always running from place to place," she said. "This place used to be a park and it has that kind of a feel; it's a place where people can come and relax."

Within its walls, the Beer Garden has more than 100 picnic benches situated among the 20 old-growth trees. Festive lights strung between the trees and a small center stage for live entertainment help to give the space an old European village feel. The picnic tables have sparked both romantic and business connections, which is the true spirit of any beer garden—a place to meet new people and spend time with family and friends. Some locals have been coming here with their families since they were children. Special event festivals are also common; the Beer Garden's Oktoberfest is known as one of the best in the city.

The Bohemian Hall and Beer Garden was built in 1910 on what was then a cow pasture. It was created by the Bohemian Citizens Benevolent Society, a fraternal organization where Bohemian men (now latter-day Czechs) would meet, socialize, and do business. Women were soon brought into the fold, hosting and attending numerous events, including festivals and dances. Later, the public was invited to enjoy this "Little Prague" and other immigrant groups—including Hungarians, Italians, and Irish—also found it to be a home away from home.

Now, after all these decades, the Beer Garden still packs them in. On its best days, the staff can serve 1,600 people at one time. The place has such a following that it stays open as long as visitors can bear the cold months. Then, it is off to the indoor bar and restaurant, which is open year-

BEER GARDEN
AT BOHEMIAN HALL

WAITRESS
SERVICE
AVAILABLE

NO
BEER GAMES
PERMITTED

ČESKÝ DOMOV

round. The restaurant's cuisine—an authentic menu of traditional, home-cooked Czech and Slovak dishes created by a chef formally trained in Europe—helps keep the Bohemian Hall and Beer Garden's Czech culture alive.

The food—especially the slow-cooked goulash—is delicious, but the Beer Garden is really all about the beer. At any given time, it offers 14 different kinds, and these aren't your run-of-the-mill brews. The Beer Garden takes pride in offering an eclectic selection of European beers, with a heavy emphasis on Czech and Slovakian varieties. Plus, to stay true to the spirit of a beer garden, it supports local breweries in Brooklyn, Long Island, and upstate New York. On good weekends, it can go through 400 kegs of beer, sometimes even causing its local beer distributors to run out of their product.

The Beer Garden is only part of this place's special history, though. The Bohemian Hall next door is also busy with its share of events, many of which are funded by the revenue generated from the Beer Garden. After all these years, the hall is still a community center for Czech immigrants. There is a school to teach children about Czech language and history, and gymnastics classes, an important part of Czech culture. For the adults, there are outreach programs, classes, and social events that include live performances and special guest speakers. For example, former Czech Republic president Václav Havel visited in 1989.

As the years go by, more than just Czechs are finding this oasis to be a special place. Many new immigrant groups in the neighborhood—like Muslims and Hindus—now rent it for parties and festivals. All of this helps to continue to preserve the Bohemian Hall and Beer Garden's true mission: a place for friends and family to meet, mingle, and relax—no matter what their origins.

CAMEO PET SHOP

Established in 1947

11523 Jamaica Avenue
Richmond Hill, Queens
718-849-6678
Subway: E train to Jamaica–Van Wyck
Open Monday–Saturday:
12:00 p.m. to 6:00 p.m.
Sunday: 12:00 p.m. to 4:00 p.m.

In this age of big-box chain stores, it is no small feat for a family-owned pet shop to sit on the same street corner for more than six decades. Cameo Pet Shop in Richmond Hill, Queens, has done just that. People come from all over New York City and Long Island for the shop's unique stock and expert advice, particularly when it comes to freshwater aquariums. The reason for Cameo's success is Steve Gruebel, who first began working here as a young man. Now, he is the owner and one of the foremost freshwater aquarium experts in the Northeast.

Cameo Pet Shop was opened by Gruebel's ex-wife's father and grandfather back in 1947. Back then, it was the thing to name your store after something well-known in the neighborhood. The very popular Casino Movie Palace was nearby, so the original owners wanted to name it after that. "Problem was, when my ex-wife's grandfather went downtown to register the business, he forgot the name and called it Cameo instead," said Gruebel, laughing.

For many, part of the enjoyment of shopping at Cameo Pet Shop is its decor, which is a time warp back to the 1950s. There's the '50s-style wood paneling, vintage shop signs, gleaming vintage stainless-steel aquariums, and heavy-gauge metal birdcages, many of which are collector's items. Gruebel was going to remodel about 20 years ago, but the customers talked him out of it. Many said that Cameo is the only thing in the neighborhood that hasn't changed since their childhoods.

Nostalgia aside, Cameo has always been known for having some of the best freshwater aquarium fish and supplies around. Dozens of beautiful tanks line the store. The fish and their surroundings are carefully picked out, creating dazzling aquatic displays. Like a true specialist in any field, Gruebel is a bit obsessive. "I go down and handpick the fish," he said. "I don't do it on the phone; I pick every fish in person. I make sure they give me the best they have."

One customer, aquarium enthusiast Herb Walgren, thinks Gruebel's extensive knowledge is essential. "True aquarists want to replicate nature," he said. "Steve specializes in live plants. Most shops don't really have live plants anymore." And you certainly won't find Walgren in a chain pet store. He laments that maintaining a freshwater aquarium is quickly becoming a lost art. "There is so much to know. What kind

of fish should live together, their specialty foods, what plants are beneficial to the tank, all these things," he said. Gruebel is so good at the art that he is able to create aquariums that are literally self-sustaining mini-ecosystems.

Need more proof of Gruebel's expertise? Look no further than the story of Cameo's pet fish, Buttkiss, an 18-inch South American Pacu fish. After being returned by a customer who complained that the fish grew too large for its tank, Buttkiss lived at Cameo for more than 40 years. Gruebel said he did nothing special except care for the fish properly, giving it a diet of six or so goldfish per day. Oh, how Buttkiss loved goldfish. When he was hungry, Buttkiss would bang on the top of the aquarium lid until he was fed, which scarred his nose over the years.

In recent years, Buttkiss became a bit of a celebrity, even making international news. It all started when an Internet blog caught wind of his longevity and posted a story about him. Soon, other media outlets came calling, including National Public Radio, the New York Daily News, and even a newspaper in India. "It didn't help business one bit," said Gruebel, laughing. "Oh well, it was a fun ride." It was also a last hurrah for Buttkiss, for he went to the big aquarium in the sky in early 2011. Gruebel's son had the fish stuffed by a taxidermist, and he now hangs on the wall at Cameo.

Gruebel also likes to tell the story of a nice little old lady who came in with her canary several years ago, asking if he could help it feel better. "We looked in the box and it was obviously dead," said Gruebel. "I nudged my then-brother-in-law and said, 'What's that red band around the stomach?' We thought it must be a Lutino canary, but then we looked at the woman and saw her red lipstick. She had put the bird in her mouth and tried to resuscitate it. Talk about eccentric!"

With stories like these, it's no wonder why Cameo has established a reputation as not only a great place to buy pet supplies, but also one of those old neighborhood places where people go to hang out, chew the fat, and catch up on area gossip. In fact, one regular customer is Pat Polisciano, a spry World War II veteran who lives upstairs. He has never even owned a pet.

EDDIE'S SWEET SHOP

Established in the 1920s

10529 Metropolitan Avenue, Forest Hills, Queens
www.facebook.com/eddiessweetshop 718-520-8514
Subway: E or F train to 75th Avenue
Open Tuesday–Friday: 1:00 p.m. to 11:30 p.m.
Saturday–Sunday: 12:00 p.m. to 11:30 p.m.

One thing woefully missing from small-town America these days is the old-fashioned ice cream parlor. Sure, there are plenty of chains—Dairy Queen, Carvel, and Baskin-Robbins, for example—but none exude the classic feel, not to mention taste, of a one-of-a-kind ice cream parlor. Forest Hills, Queens, is lucky, for Eddie's Sweet Shop has been providing the neighborhood with such a place for a century.

"You come in here and you get great ambiance, and we also make the ice cream just like it was many years ago," said owner Vito Citrano. The Citranos are the fourth owners of this little ice cream parlor on the corner, which seems like it has been around forever. Customers from four or five generations continue to visit the store. In fact, even though they've had the shop for about 45 years, old timers still call the Citranos the "new owners."

No one is quite sure exactly how old the parlor is, but most agree it has been in business almost 100 years. Back in the early 1900s, refrigeration was a luxury. One couldn't pop down to the local store to buy a gallon of ice cream. Places like Eddie's were a special treat, not only a respite from the daily grind, but also a communal place for the neighborhood.

Eddie's itself has changed little over the decades. Most of the fixtures inside are antique, but are still used daily. The refrigerator is more than 75 years old and was one of the first to use electricity. The cash register is so old its keys only go up to $5. The cast-iron short stools bellied up to the white marble counter, the vintage ice cream advertisements, the dainty metal ice cream saucers, the inlayed wood bar—everything adds to the throwback experience at Eddie's.

The authenticity of Eddie's Sweet Shop has not gone unnoticed by Hollywood. Several commercials and movies have been shot here, including Neil Simon's *Brighton Beach Memoirs*. Citrano confided that not all the shoots were glamorous, though. During one of the movies—he won't reveal which—the crew dropped a camera on the original marble counter, cracking it. "We're going to leave it there. In about 20 or 30 years, it will be a funny story," said Citrano. "Right now it's still not a funny story. It still really hurts."

Artifacts aside, the real draw of Eddie's is its ice cream. All 20 flavors are made from scratch in-house in the basement kitchen. The flavors are classics like strawberry, vanilla, and rum raisin. "Most of our ice cream flavors are very old-fashioned," said Citrano. "We don't even have cookies and cream yet. It's getting pretty old, though, so we may start putting that on the menu." The toppings—like whipped cream and butterscotch—are all made using original recipes passed down from each owner. Like any ice cream shop worth its weight in New York City, Eddie's also makes classic beverages like egg creams, lime rickeys, and Coca-Cola made the old-fashioned way—a couple of pumps of syrup followed by a shot of seltzer. In fact, there has always been a gentleman's agreement between owners to properly train the successors with all the correct recipes and techniques.

The Citranos have been asked to open a second location, but they have refused for fear of overextending themselves and jeopardizing the quality of their products. The family will run Eddie's for as long as humanely possible. "This place means a lot to people," said Citrano. "It is important to us to keep it going."

SUNDAES

CHOC. SPRINKLE
MARSHMALLOW
HOT FUDGE
CARAMEL
BUTTERSCOTCH
PINEAPPLE TEMP.
WALNUT
BANANA SPLIT
BANANA ROYAL

Joseph Biunno is a place where furniture dreams come true. This is a place where customers can come in with just a photograph or rough sketch of a piece of furniture and the shop can create a near exact replica of it. "Many times it's cheaper to just build a piece from scratch than to buy a Chippendale piece at auction," said owner Joseph Biunno.

But soup-to-nuts furniture manufacturing is only one of Joseph Biunno's many talents. In its large workshop in Long Island City, Queens, it can fix and restore any kind of furniture, from an authentic 18th-century piece from France to Grandma's settee. Regluing, matching veneers, sanding, painting and gilding, and a variety of other techniques—all of it is old hat to Joseph Biunno. Self-taught, Biunno even fabricates antique keys that have been lost to time for doors and wood cabinets.

Like many businesses, the holiday season is a busy one for Joseph Biunno, but it's due to more unusual circumstances. Biunno calls it "Chair Season." "Everybody is entertaining and dragging chairs out for the extra company. Chairs get dented or arms or legs may crack, so right after Thanksgiving we get a pretty good influx of small little repairs to get people ready for Christmas."

JOSEPH BIUNNO

Established in 1958

21-07 Borden Avenue
Long Island City, Queens
www.antiquefurnitureusa.com
718-729-5630
Subway: 7 train to Hunters Point Avenue
Open Monday–Friday:
9:00 a.m. to 5:00 p.m.

Sometimes restoring a particular piece of furniture is more expensive than replacing it, but sentimental value often wins out. Biunno regularly sees furniture just waiting to be brought back to its former glory, pieces brimming with old-world craftsmanship, made with rare materials like ivory or hard-as-rock old-growth wood too precious to throw out.

Joseph Biunno is also adept at creating decorative curtain finials and rods, and is nationally known for its unique and abundant stock. "Our showroom has been described as a candy store for drapery treatments," said Biunno. And rightly so, for it has some 500 different sets, including everything from monkey and elephant heads to roaring flames and ornate stars.

Next to the finial showroom is the actual workshop. Specialized tools of all shapes and sizes line the walls. Each section of the shop is dedicated to one discipline, including painting, welding, turning, and polishing. Workers each have their own specialty, skills like water gilding, composite casting, and high-gloss French polishing. Even sanding is a specialty relegated to one man. Many of Joseph Biunno's employees are from Europe. "It's a different mentality over there as far as education goes. They respect the shop arts much more. I know one gentleman who went to school in Italy and was basically the town hero because he was the No. 1 cabinet maker in school," said Biunno.

Thanks in part to all that talent, Joseph Biunno has been featured in just about every home-decorating magazine, including *House and Garden*, *House Beautiful*, *World of Interiors*, *Veranda*, and *Estate*. Its client list also features a who's who of celebrities, including Woody Allen, Madonna, and Denzel Washington.

The business began in essence with Joseph Biunno's grandfather, Giuseppe Biunno, a furniture artisan from Naples, Italy, who immigrated to America in 1908. Working for some of the best furniture manufacturers in New York City, he was always continually honing his craft. Eventually he passed his skills on to his son, Joseph, who opened his own small workshop in 1958. Joseph's son—also named Joseph—came into the business in 1973, working there during the weekends and after school. He then took over the business in 1985 and has been there ever since, helping people enjoy their cherished pieces of furniture while preserving the best in craftsmanship in New York City.

These days, movie theaters are mostly run by corporate conglomerates, but there was a time when many theaters were mom-and-pops, often owned by someone in the neighborhood. Kew Gardens Cinemas is one such place, and one of just a handful of independently owned theaters left in New York City.

"It's got that down-home feeling, like theaters from yesteryear," said one regular customer. That's just what owner Harvey Elgart hopes customers take away from his classic theater in Kew Gardens, Queens. Customers often say that it reminds them of what it was like to go to the movies when they were young, when everyone went to the neighborhood theater. According to Elgart, once people try the Kew Gardens experience, they no longer have any desire to go to a corporate multiplex.

Kew Gardens Cinemas was originally named the Austin Theater, built in the 1930s as part of the Rugoff theater chain. Up until the 1960s, the theater showed first-run films and art films. In the 1970s, a new owner started showing pornographic films and basically ran the theater into the ground. Elgart took over in 1998 and began the long process of restoring it.

Walk into Kew Gardens and right away you'll see the difference between a chain theater and what is clearly a labor of love. Renovations revealed a number of treasures, including the original interior designed by Harold Rambusch, who also decorated Radio City Music Hall. "The cove ceiling and original murals that are in the lobby were buried under the hung ceiling," said Elgart. "All of the brick walls and all of the woodworking were buried behind sheetrock." In fact, when Elgart bought the theater, he thought the ceiling was dark green instead of its actual color—the accumulation of cigarette smoke over the years had stained it 10 shades deeper.

For better or for worse, modernity has prevented a few of the original fixtures from going back up. Elgart has the original Art Deco cut-glass entrance doors, but he could not put them in the theater because they don't meet modern standards for safety glass. Original doors aside, there are plenty of other special touches, for the theater is a miniature museum of Elgart's original movie collectibles. The walls are lined with classic film posters from the 1940s, '50s, and '60s. The concession stand even serves homemade cookies.

It's not just the movie memorabilia and old-time feel that keeps moviegoers coming back, though. Elgart is quite capable of holding his own against corporate theaters, selling tickets at lower prices than Manhattan theaters while providing the same amenities, such as cushy seats and state-of-the-art pictures and sound. Plus, by being independent, Elgart can be choosy about what plays here. "This theater is strictly art, independent, and foreign films, and little obscure titles that you wouldn't find anywhere else," he said. "We're very selective in what we play." Sometimes Elgart makes decisions about what movies to show that aren't necessarily the best for profit, but he'd rather show good films than sell out.

Today, as the neighborhood around Kew Gardens continues to grow in popularity, business for the theater is better than ever. It is also available for special events like film festivals and independent film premieres. In fact, Elgart holds quite a few independent film screenings at Kew Gardens and its sister theater in Brooklyn, Cobble Hill Cinemas. One recent example is *The Cake Eaters*, directed by Mary Stuart Masterson. In 2008, Elgart even added two more auditoriums on the second floor of Kew Gardens, something unheard of for an independent theater to do in this era.

"Every day's a new day because with every new film, it feels like it's something new in your life and new business to get excited about," said Elgart.

KEW GARDENS CINEMAS

Established in 1998

81–05 Lefferts Boulevard
Kew Gardens, Queens
www.kewgardenstheatre.com
718-441-9835
Subway: E or F train
to Kew Gardens–Union Turnpike
Open daily at 12:30 p.m.
The theater has late shows on
Friday and Saturday evenings.

VANILLA CHIP CHOCOLATE
WATERMELON ALMOND
Orange-Vanilla Cherry-Vanilla
PEANUT BUTTER COFFEE
SUGAR FREE

HATS
$15.00

SHIRTS
$8.00
XXL $10.00

ITALIAN ICES

CUPS

PRICE LIST
ALL TAXES INCLUDED

INSULATE BAGS FOR
Containers Only 1.00

PINT
500

QUART
700

SMALL MEDIUM LARGE SUPER
1.50 2.00 2.50 3.00

WE DO NOT MIX
OR EXCHANGE ICES

CANS, RETAIL - WHOLESALE • INSULATED BAGS
• OPEN NIGHTLY TILL

THE LEMON ICE KING OF CORONA

Established in the 1940s

5202 108th Street, Corona, Queens
www.thelemonicekingofcorona.com 718-699-5133
Subway: 7 train to 111th Street
Open Sunday–Thursday: 10:00 a.m. to 11:00 p.m.
Friday–Saturday: 10:00 a.m. to 12:00 a.m.

During the summer, Italian ice is sold on just about every street corner in New York City, but some people go all the way to Corona, Queens, for it. The reason? Queens is where to find the king—the Lemon Ice King of Corona, that is. The Lemon Ice King is one of those mom-and-pop institutions that all true New Yorkers know about. It is famous for one thing and one thing only: Italian ices.

The Lemon Ice King of Corona was first opened in the 1940s by Nicholas Benfaremo. His son, Pete, quickly joined the business, building it up to what it is today. A chef by trade, Pete Benfaremo was very particular about what went into his ices, throwing out whole batches if something was not quite right. Apparently, he knew what he was doing, for this place has received some serious accolades, including the Zagat Survey Award of Distinction, as well as several positive reviews from some of the leading food critics in America. Today's owners—Vincent Barbaccia and Michael Zampino—took over the business almost two decades ago, but only after spending years under Benfaremo's tutelage and promising him they would keep things the same. Benfaremo even continued working at the Lemon Ice King after he sold the business. He lived upstairs until he passed away in 2008.

"Pete was his own man," said Barbaccia. "I'm sure you're familiar with the Soup Nazi from *Seinfeld*? More than once it was said that he was the Lemon Ice Nazi. You got it the way he gave it to you and that was it. There was something about him, though. People were just attracted to him. He had that kind of personality." Benfaremo is dearly missed, and his personal touches are still all over the place, specifically the large red "WE DO NOT MIX" sign.

All of the Lemon Ice King of Corona's ices are made from scratch right on the premises. The shop also uses all natural ingredients. If you order lime, you are getting lime—not some bright green artificial flavoring. Barbaccia and Zampino even truck in fresh fruit and squeeze out the juice themselves. All of the recipes are top secret, with only the co-owners making the batches. "These are the recipes that were passed down to us and they're held in the highest confidence. My wife doesn't even know them," said Barbaccia.

One secret people would love to find out is how Zampino and Barbaccia are able to get such a creamy ice texture using only water. "That's the big novelty of our ices," said Barbaccia. "They're all natural, water-based ices. They have no dairy additives and are fat-free." Once customers try the Lemon Ice King, they are hooked for life. On blistering summer days, the shop can go through nearly 200 gallons of ice per day. According to Barbaccia, customers come for Italian ices even in the dead of winter, and will often complain if the shop closes early due to weather.

With roughly 40 flavors available, customers have a tough time picking a favorite. "I enjoy seeing the people coming up here for the first time," said co-owner Vincent Barbaccia. "They come up here not knowing what to expect, and I love to see the reaction on their faces when they taste a particular flavor." Most try the lemon first, though, as that is the traditional flavor. Other flavors include old standbys like orange, cherry, and watermelon, but also include more exotic offerings like licorice, peanut butter, and even cantaloupe. Zampino and Barbaccia are always experimenting with new flavors, often taking suggestions from customers, though some are a little bizarre. "We had somebody who wanted an avocado flavor," said Barbaccia. "Every time he came up here, he kept pushing it and pushing it, saying, 'When are you going to make the avocado?' Luckily, he forgot about it after a while."

The Lemon Ice King benefits from being close to Citi Field. A Mets win often brings in extra customers. But what really draws people back again and again to this ice-cold wonder is a top-notch product, with a taste that is uniquely New York. "We're still a mom-and-pop operation," Barbaccia said. "People laugh at us because we don't have a computer. We just recently got a fax machine. But the place is the way it is because of the fact that we still hold to the old-fashioned rules."

New Yorkers love their deli sandwiches. Subs, wraps, heros—whatever you call them—if you open a delicatessen in the Big Apple, you better make the sandwiches right or you will not be in business for long. That said, when a deli has been in business on the same block for more than 85 years, it is no small feat.

Located under the rumbling transit trains of Jamaica Avenue in Woodhaven, Queens, Manor Deli has quietly become a neighborhood institution. Opened around 1920 by a young man whose name has been lost to history, it was originally called Woodhaven Manor. Its specialty was—and is—traditional New York German-style deli food, with 15 to 25 different items made in-house daily, including coleslaw, chicken potpie, and stuffed cabbage.

Current owner Mark Gallagher said there is a good reason the deli has been around so long—it follows the formula set in place by a previous owner, Helmuth Bolowsky, who was very meticulous. Gallagher tries to keep the place clean and neat, and uses the same recipes that the deli has used for the past 40 years. Gallagher bought the place in 1999, but he had worked here since he was 15. Now it is a family affair, with his wife, Ildiko Gallagher, supervising the kitchen.

One of the first things you'll notice when stepping into Manor Deli is how unbelievably clean it is, from the spotless floors to the sharply dressed attendants in crisp paper hats and ties. "The cleaning of the store is a daily ritual," said Gallagher. "We probably spend as many man-hours cleaning the store as we do producing products. The store is known for cleanliness. As soon as the store's not clean anymore, we're out of business."

But it is the food that sets Manor Deli apart from other delis in New York. Much of what it serves is made from scratch each day, which is quite a rarity in this prepackaged, franchised world. One of the items Manor Deli is particularly well-known for is its potato salad. "People come from all over the country to buy potato salad from us," said Gallagher. "They'll come with soup containers and say, 'Can you fill these up? We're going back to Florida.' Nobody has potato salad like this anymore. We buy hundreds of pounds of potatoes, we peel them daily, we cut them by hand, and we put in our spices. This is the way homemade food is supposed to taste."

Another popular item is the deli's egg custards. "It's a sensitive item," said Ildiko. "You have to be really careful—it can't be overbaked or underbaked—but it's really delicious and nutritious." Before dessert, however, you have to try another Manor Deli favorite—its roast beef sandwiches. The employees cook the meat in-house using only the top sides of beef. The deli is so serious about its roast beef that three different cuts are always on display so customers can pick their favorite.

Like any place that has been in business this long, Manor Deli has a few tales to tell, including the night the lights went out in 1977. "For years, we had our own generator here. During the 1977 blackout, we were the only store with cold beer and soda, and we were 100 percent operational, even the air conditioning worked," said Gallagher.

The Gallaghers are now feeding Queens residents in other neighborhoods as well. They recently opened Manor Oktoberfest restaurants in Forest Hills and at Atlas Park in Glendale. Wayne Ruggiere, a loyal customer, summed up the Manor experience: "No disrespect to Subway or a lot of the chain stores, but it's really what I consider industrial food," he said. "They don't have pride in what they make or how they make it. The food at Manor Deli is made fresh every day and a lot of pride and work goes into it."

MANOR DELICATESSEN

Established in 1920

9412 Jamaica Avenue
Woodhaven, Queens
www.manordeli.com 718-849-2836
Subway: J or Z train
to Woodhaven Boulevard
Open Monday: 7:00 a.m. to 3:00 p.m.
Tuesday–Friday: 7:00 a.m. to 8:00 p.m.
Saturday: 8:00 a.m. to 7:00 p.m.
Sunday: 9:00 a.m. to 5:00 p.m.

MICHΛEL DAVIS GLASS

Established in 1991

4224 Ninth Street, Long Island City, Queens
www.michaeldavisstainedglass.com 718-383-3712
Subway: F train to 21st Street–Queensbridge
Open by appointment only

"It is really extraordinary. I can't think of any other thing that can be nothing and five minutes later be something," said Michael Davis, owner of one of the very few glass foundries left in New York City, a place once known internationally for its glass artisans.

Today, a shop like Michael Davis Glass is one of both tradition and necessity, for the world of glassmaking is one that cannot be dramatically changed or streamlined by computers or other technology. To this day, it is an artisanal craft that must be done by a human because, like humans, it is unpredictable and always evolving.

In a nutshell, Michael Davis Glass does repairs, restorations, fabrications, and full design and execution of custom glass projects. The shop does glassblowing, casting, and bending, and even makes stained glass in its foundry in Long Island City, Queens. Projects are all over the board—from restoring original light fixtures for a historic building and creating displays for the famed Macy's store windows to repairing Grandma's irreplaceable candy jar—and new challenges are always coming through the doors.

Clients too come from all walks of life—there are independent artists, large architecture firms, interior designers, and private homeowners. And, surprisingly, they're not all from New York City. Michael Davis Glass has clients from as far away as Dubai. "That's kind of a downside, actually," said Davis. "Unless a client sends me pictures, I don't often get to see the piece in its intended setting and see the true result."

One of the Dubai projects is a great example of how Davis and his handful of employees work as a seamless team. It involved fabricating several hundred different colored fluted glass pieces as parts for an enormous chandelier designed for a retail mall. The process was complicated—each piece had to be colored, heated, and blown—all the while working with materials that were at temperatures of more than 2,000 degrees. When finished, the pieces were cooled in an annealer to bring the glass to room temperature.

Restorations are just as challenging and just as enjoyable for Davis. Recently, he began reproducing turn-of-the-century etched-glass shades for a renovated Washington, D.C., government building. "It's like CSI," he said. "You got a 'body' (the shade) and you are diagnosing it. You look at all the tool and shell marks and whatever else is on that piece and try to get a good sense of how it was produced. The learning never ends." Davis can spend months on a reproduction just getting his "head around it"—that is, figuring out the techniques and executions of the old glass masters.

Like many New Yorkers, Davis's career path diverged from his original plans. He first came to the city as a modern dancer and did stained-glass work as a day job. Stained glass is a particular specialty; he apprenticed with master stained-glass restorer Jack Cushen, which led to restoration jobs on church windows made by Louis Comfort Tiffany. He also created blown glass pieces on the side, which he sold at Barney's and Tiffany and Co. That steady work gave him the confidence and ability to open up his own studio in 1991. He's been going strong ever since, and he still finds interest in his work. "My work has sort of an inevitable evolution that leads to wherever the final piece is meant to be," he said.

Union Course
Fishing Club
Meets Here
First Tues of
Every Month

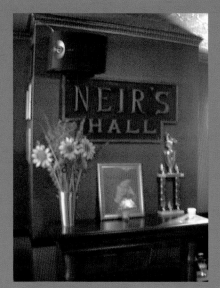

NEIR'S
HALL

WELCOME

NEIR'S TAVERN & STEAKHOUSE

Established in 1829

8748 78th Street, Woodhaven, Queens
www.neirstavern.com 718-296-0600
Subway: J or Z train to 75th Street
Open Monday–Saturday:
11:00 a.m. to 2:00 a.m.
Sunday: 11:00 a.m. to 12:00 a.m.

This could be the most famous New York City bar you have never heard of—a place thick with history and stories both modern and old, not to mention bragging rights to an eclectic group of performers. Neir's Tavern is located in one of the last places one would expect to find a bar, but it has been there for generations. Tucked away on a quiet residential street in Woodhaven, Queens, the tavern strangely does not look out of place. Perhaps that is its appeal. It is a true neighborhood bar that has survived by word-of-mouth advertising its entire life.

As the oldest bar in Queens and one of the oldest in the country, the place opened in 1829. It began as the "Blue Pump Room," named unceremoniously after a nearby water pump. The reason for its location made sense at the time; right across the street stood one of the preeminent horse racing tracks in America: the Union Course. The track's reputation was legendary. "In 1823, the Union Course had a race where 70,000 people came. The city of New York was empty because so many people had come to see this race between a Northern horse and a Southern horse," said co-owner Alex Ewen. The track was a good neighbor to Neir's,

keeping the tavern packed with patrons. Never a high-end establishment, it was the kind of place where the stable boys and jockeys went after work.

By the 1890s the racetrack was gone, but the tavern carried on through the decades, reinventing itself as Neir's Social Hall, which catered to local immigrants. Balls and events were put on regularly. Upstairs was a hotel, rumored to do double-duty as a brothel. Live entertainment was also popular. Among the entertainers, musicians, and vaudevillians was one actress in particular: Mae West. She got her start as a singer here when she was just 10 years old. Once she hit it big, she frequented the bar with friends, one of which was W. C. Fields.

After changing hands several times over the years, the place slowly began to fall apart. In 1980, the place suffered major fire damage, rumored to be arson stemming from a dispute between owners. In fact, the mahogany bar still has scorch marks from the fire. The tavern lingered on until it caught the eye of movie director Martin Scorsese, who is the reason that Neir's looks so familiar to so many people. Scorsese shot several key scenes here for his classic 1990 film *Goodfellas*. Fans of the film are pleasantly surprised to see that little has changed inside since the movie was shot.

But unfortunately, its movie connection was not enough to keep the place—then called Union Course Tavern—afloat. It struggled on until just a few years ago when a group of investors committed to preserving this great piece of history came in. Their first order of business was to renovate the place without disturbing its wonderful patina. During this time, they found several hidden gems—like period furniture and gaslight fixtures—which they retrofitted for electricity. They also found the remnants of a bowling alley in the back, quite possibly one of the first in the United States. In the basement, they found wood structural beams with tree bark still on them, which helped to confirm the stories that the wood was salvaged from the original Union Course Race-track stables.

But the best item from the good old days is the beer tap system, which was installed more than 100 years ago. Using no electricity, the tap's metal coils are packed daily in ice, and then the beer is pumped through them. The new owners considered putting in a modern tap system, but a beverage distributer talked them out of it, saying the old system actually lends itself to colder beer.

Ice-cold beer is not the only thing keeping Neir's open, though. Today's owners have brought the bar back to its roots as a kind of modern-day social hall. There are now renovated apartments upstairs, a martial arts school in one of the original ballrooms, and even a recording studio, which has a history of its own. "I recorded most of Salt-n-Pepa's albums here, most of Kid 'n Play's records. I recorded Kiss, Anthrax, Eminem. The list goes on and on," said co-owner David Eng. Perhaps taking a cue from Mae West, Eng now uses Neir's as a place to showcase his new talent—the tavern features live music on most nights.

Today, Neir's Tavern is much like the rest of the city—a place that reinvents itself over and over again. "If you come here, sit down, and talk to these people you start to realize that this is just a tight-knit community. Eventually what happens is they start to share their stories and you start to become part of the Neir's family as well," said co-owner Loycent Gordon.

UNION COURSE
THE BLUE PUMP RM OPENED 1855
RENAMED FOR THE RACETRACK A
HOTEL THEATER MAE WEST PER-
FORMED & SCORSESE FILMED GOOD-
FELLOWS HERE RENAMED NIERS

WOODHAVEN CULT. & HISTORICAL SOC.

Halloween comes and goes every year and then most people don't really think about it. That is, unless you're part of the Beige family from Woodhaven, Queens. Living and working out of the same building in the 1950s, Rubie's Costume Company has gone on to become one of the largest costume companies in the world, operating in 15 countries and employing 2,600 people worldwide. Rubie's makes costumes of every kind—from inexpensive kids' costumes to extravagant, multi-layered ones for adults. Today, Rubie's produces 10,000 different items for Halloween alone.

"My father Rubin and mother Tillie actually started the company back in 1951," said executive vice president Howard Beige. "It was started as a novelty company that sold mostly tricks and jokes, and eventually my parents started to get calls for costumes, which they started to manufacture themselves." Today, the company's costumes are sold everywhere from specialty shops to big-box chain stores. Retailers from around the world come to see the company's latest offerings at its wholesale showroom in Manhattan, affectionately known as the "Halloween Tower."

Through the years, Rubie's has even outfitted a few iconic figures. It has created costumes for the General Mills corporation characters, like the Kool-Aid Man, and Fruit of the Loom characters for traveling shows and commercials. In 1976, Rubie's outfitted the U.S. Army in period costumes to celebrate the country's bicentennial.

All of the company's costume lines are created in-house by designers, many of which come from Manhattan's high-end fashion industry. And with so much manufacturing going overseas these days, Rubie's is committed to making as many costumes as possible in the United States. A lot of the work is still done in the Richmond Hill factory, a place buzzing with activity. Each sewing machine operator can produce between 20 and 40 costumes per day.

RUBIE'S COSTUME COMPANY

Established in 1951

120-08 Jamaica Avenue
Richmond Hill, Queens
www.rubies.com
718-846-1008
Subway: J or Z train
to 121st Street
Open Monday–Friday:
10:00 a.m. to 6:00 p.m.
Peak season is September
through December.
Hours and days may vary.

Keeping with its family-oriented company principles, costume-makers start at 7:30 a.m. so they can be home for their children after school. Keeping the employees happy is a smart move, for this is far from a seasonal business. "I can tell you that our business requires 365 days a year of work. We are supplying the U.S. market for holidays such as Christmas, New Year's, St. Patrick's Day, Easter, summer luaus—a wide variety of events," said Beige.

But the company's biggest holiday is still Halloween, which over the last 20 years has become big business. Up until the late 1970s and early 1980s, children's costumes were typically made of vinyl, plastic, or very inexpensive rayon. "Sometime in the very early '80s there were all these Halloween scares out there about razors in apples and everything else," said Beige. "For a few years, Halloween started to move indoors. These better costumes became very popular because if you were sending your children to a party and they were competing for a prize, you generally chose not to send them in a $3.99 plastic costume. So Halloween became a little bit more competitive and a little more fashion-oriented."

Over the years political masks have become very popular. Since Halloween is typically seven to 10 days before Election Day, Rubie's can often predict the winner of the upcoming race. The best-selling political mask is usually the winner.

Not only is Rubie's constantly putting out new costumes, it is also experimenting with new technology. One such innovation, for the company's masks, uses very soft latex that moves with the person's face, creating a more authentic look.

And as Rubie's keeps its eyes on the future, with the third generation now joining the ranks, the company also remembers its roots. "I think my mother and father would marvel at the fact that this is a company that employs 2,600 people worldwide and yet it is still a family company run with family values."

SCHMIDT'S CANDY

Established in 1925

9415 Jamaica Avenue, Woodhaven, Queens
www.schmidtscandy.com 718-846-9326
Subway: J or Z train to Woodhaven Boulevard
Open Tuesday–Saturday: 11:00 a.m. to 6:00 p.m.
Closed Sunday and Monday
Closed during July and August

Under the rumbling transit trains of Jamaica Avenue in Woodhaven, Queens, sits a lost slice of Europe, a place where the candies are so unique one would be hard-pressed to find them anywhere else in New York City. It is Schmidt's Candy, one of the only places in Queens still making most of its sweets in-house and by hand. The shop uses old-world European techniques that are labor-intensive and painfully sensitive to the elements, but they are oh-so-worth the trouble.

Margie Schmidt is the third-generation owner and candy maker-in-chief, and she creates most of the sweets herself. According to Schmidt, the place has always been an old favorite in the neighborhood. "A lot of people have moved away and they'll come back for holidays and then they get to relive part of their youth," she said. "It's like a step back in time."

The history of Schmidt's is a classic New York tale. Margie Schmidt's grandfather opened the shop in 1925 and lived upstairs with his wife and six children. His specialty was bringing original German chocolate recipes to the area and using old-world techniques. Margie, who took the reins

from her parents in 1986, has worked here since she was a child. "I'm now the only grandchild left in the business," she said. "As a kid, I had to help my father stir the chocolate; I had to cut the caramels; I had to scrape the jellybeans off the floor when they spilled. I'm still doing it all."

Respecting tradition and just plain good taste, Schmidt sticks with her grandfather's original recipes and in many cases uses his original candy-making tools, including copper kettles and cast-iron candy molds that are now collectors' items. In fact, Schmidt is so dedicated to tradition and quality that she actually closes the shop in the summer because the pure ingredients don't work well with hot weather. "You can't compare our caramel to a Kraft caramel. We're closed all summer because there's nothing in the caramels but milk, heavy cream, butter, and sugar, and therefore it doesn't last. In every other kind of candy, there is a list of preservatives a mile long, but here it's butter, sugar, milk, corn syrup, and cream. You can taste the difference," she explained.

Dozens of sweet offerings are on display in the antique glass and wood display cabinets at the shop, most of which

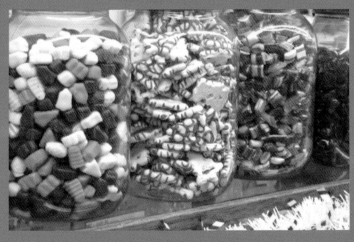

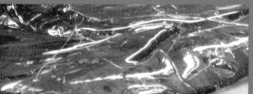

are original from when Schmidt's first opened in the 1920s. The store's specialty is chocolates and confections that include caramels, hard candies, and marzipan. All of the chocolates are hand-dipped to ensure quality and to make sure just the right amount of chocolate covers each filling, something Schmidt said a machine couldn't duplicate as well. Fillings include creams, like maple and raspberry; fruits, like coconut and pineapple; and jellies, nuts, and fudges. Schmidt dips the chocolates herself, adding small designs to the top of each piece, and then allows the candy to cool on wooden racks.

If dipping chocolate is a hard-learned skill, then making ribbon candy and candy canes is a Ph.D. All of the ribbon candy is hand-pulled, and as far as Schmidt knows, she's the only one in New York City still doing it this way. She starts by boiling pure cane sugar in a copper kettle. Once it is liquefied, she pours it out on a marble counter. While it cools and becomes malleable, she adds flavoring and coloring.

Then, she hangs the candy on a hook on the wall in order to pull it. Last, she cuts the finished candy into shapes.

Schmidt's unique candies are not the only reason people come back decade after decade. There is another lost pleasure here: customer service. It is one of those places where the business owner actually knows and waits on the customers. For example, one customer came in recently and asked Schmidt for a gift for his grandmother. Schmidt put the gift together in a box, and then wrapped it. Surprised, the man said, "You don't have to wrap it. It's only for my grandmother." Schmidt immediately replied, "You must not be Italian. You don't give Grandma a box without wrapping it."

This is just one of the reasons why New York City needs places likes Schmidt's. "These days everything is mass-marketed, everything is BJ's, everything is warehouses. There is no contact," said Schmidt. "You want to go in a store, you want to smell the chocolate. That's a pleasant experience."

TISH & SNOOKY'S MANIC PANIC

Established in 1977

21-07 Borden Avenue, Long Island City, Queens
www.manicpanic.com 718-937-6055
Subway: 7 train to Hunters Point Avenue
Open Monday–Friday: 9:00 a.m. to 5:00 p.m.

In Queens, there are two sisters known as the "Martha Stewarts of Punk." Meet Tish and Snooky Bellomo, purveyors of punk fashion and founders of Manic Panic, a cosmetics and hair color company famously known for its extreme colors and concepts. The first of its kind, Manic Panic's authentic punk roots and sensibility are, believe it or not, the epitome of an American success story. "We grew up really poor, raised just by our single mother, and now we have this huge business. I don't know where else in the world that could happen," said Snooky Bellomo.

With sales in the millions, Manic Panic products are everywhere from hair salons, tattoo parlors, and record stores to national chain stores like Hot Topic and Spencer Gifts. There is even a stand-alone shop in Hollywood, California, two licensed salons in Fresno and Highland Park, California, and a boutique at the headquarters in Long Island City, Queens. The shops sell a range of cosmetics like lipstick, foundation, eye shadow, and false eyelashes with names to suit their eclectic colors: Vampire Red, Green Envy, and Electric Lizard. Hair color is Manic Panic's signature product, including colors like Electric Lava, Fuchsia Shock, and Voodoo Blue.

"It's the best quality and it's gentle on the hair. Our dyes are really more vibrant than any of the other knock-off brands. They're not garish; they're gorgeous," said Tish Bellomo. "Plus, it's made by punk rockers. It's the real deal.

We don't just sell it, we live it, we wear it. It's something we care about."

Tish and Snooky are indeed authentic. They began their colorful odyssey as musicians, becoming the back-up singers in the original line-up for the band Blondie. Taking a page from the emerging punk scene of London, they began wearing bright hair colors, which they found were not widely accepted even in the freewheeling days of 1970s New York City. "Somebody once came over to me and punched me in the face," said Tish. Snooky was not immune, either. "I had a guy in a Rolls-Royce roll down his window and say, 'You know, you look absolutely ridiculous, absolutely ridiculous. He had to say it twice to make sure I got it. But who is ridiculous now?" she said.

Singers Katy Perry, Lady Gaga, and the godmother of outrageous glam—Cyndi Lauper—all use Manic Panic hair color. Singer Rihanna does, too, using a secret mixture of reds that only her hairdresser knows for sure. Men also use Manic Panic products, including basketball player Dennis Rodman and singer Marilyn Manson, who uses the Virgin White powder. Manic Panic hair color has also been seen in movies like *Eternal Sunshine of the Spotless Mind* and *Whip It*, and the television show *Gilmore Girls*.

Back in the 1970s, friends began asking the sisters about their hair color and cosmetics, so they decided to open up a shop on St. Mark's Place in the East Village. The sisters'

Tish & Snooky's Manic Panic 22nd Anniversary

Better Red Than Dead

mother, who they cite as their inspiration, came up with the name for the company. "We were trying to think of a name and she was working in a mental hospital at the time. Her manic-depressive patients would go into what they called "manic panics." She thought that would be a good name, and we agreed," said Snooky.

As the first punk style boutique in America, it soon became a mecca for the lifestyle. The sisters put everything into it, even rummaging through dumpsters of the department store where Snooky used to work to retrieve discarded mannequins. During the day they tended shop, sometimes only making 25 cents in sales. At night, they performed on stage at nearby CBGB as one of the original punk bands in New York—The Sick F**ks—and opened for groups like The Ramones and Television. In 1989, a drastic rent increase forced them to close the East Village shop. "Our landlord actually did us a favor, because it caused us to concentrate on the wholesale side of the business. We built it to what it is today," said Tish.

Manic Panic's company headquarters in Queens looks more like a college dorm than the shining example of a successful capitalist venture that it is. Original rock playbills line the walls; there's a zebra print couch in the lobby; and Tish's dachshund wanders the halls. Employees wear the company's products proudly while hovering over computers and consulting corporate vendors. So do the sisters have any conflicts between their punk sensibilities and corporate ties? "No, not really," said Tish. "We run the business on our terms. We don't do animal testing and only use high-quality products."

So exactly what is the appeal of coloring one's hair such bright colors? Sure, sociologists have their various theories, but according to Tish and Snooky, it is just plain fun. "It's a harmless way of expressing yourself and rebelling. I don't want to make some grand statement, but many people tell us how they changed their hair color and it made them more confident, self-assured, and happy," said Snooky. "One time, there was an 80-year-old woman in Canada who said she felt invisible because nobody wanted to talk to her," added Tish. "She dyed her hair purple and she said now people want to have their picture taken with her. It really changed her life for the better."

Bigelow

BRO

Holter

Killmeyer's

Old Bavaria Inn

KENNY'S
CASTAWAY

Hotel

STATEN ISLAND

BROWNIES PRO AND SPORT HOBBIES

Established in 1971

124 Bennett Street, Port Richmond, Staten Island
www.brownieshobbies.com 718-727-2194
Bus: S53, S57, S59, or S66
to Port Richmond Avenue–Bennett Street
Open Tuesday–Wednesday: 12:00 p.m. to 6:00 p.m.
Thursday–Friday: 12:00 p.m. to 9:00 p.m.
Saturday: 10:00 a.m. to 6:00 p.m.
Closed Sunday and Monday

Brownies Pro and Sport Hobbies is located on a quiet residential street in the neighborhood of Port Richmond. It's not really a place one would expect to find a hobby shop, but people all over New York City still search it out. The reason is simple: places like this—old-time hobby shops catering to hardcore hobbyists and youngsters alike—just do not exist anymore.

The little shop packs a big punch, for it is filled floor-to-ceiling with every kind of hobby imaginable: radio control airplanes, cars, and boats, crafts, art supplies, model kits, slot cars, and even model rockets with tiny built-in cameras. The ceiling alone is a sight to see. It is practically a mini museum, with every inch of space taken over by hundreds of model airplanes ranging from old windups from the 1920s to today's electronic ones, some even with actual miniature jet engines.

Brownies Hobbies is the culmination of one man's lifelong love of hobbies. A Staten Island native, George Brown—or "Brownie," as he's known—began his love affair with model airplanes back in the 1930s when he was just six years old. As a young man, he built aircraft models used to train fighter pilots during World War II. His wife, Mary, said even on their first date she knew right away that if you loved Brownie, you had to love his planes. "I still laugh at how many times we started to go to the movies, and he'd say to me, 'Oh, can we go down and glue a little bit of something on my airplane?' That would be the end of our movie date," she said.

Working as a tool and die machinist by day to feed his six children, Brown's dream was to own his own hobby shop. For years, he held court in the family basement, teaching others about model airplanes, giving pointers, and helping other hobbyists with their projects. After coming into a little bit of money in 1971—the grand sum of $1,300, to be exact—the Browns managed to find a place to start their hobby shop. For years, Brown continued his job as a machinist while trying to get the business off the ground. Family members often pitched in to help run the shop. Even today, the shop is a family place: Brownie and Mary run the store and live upstairs, and their son, John, manages the business end.

With today's technology, there is a hobby to fit everyone's skill level. "It's more pre-fab now," said Brownie. "In the

majority of kits, you can literally take a plane out of the box and fly it. It used to be everything was built from scratch from a print. I would even whittle the curved nose of the plane myself with a knife in those days. Now, you just buy a plastic pre-formed cone."

Fortunately for Brownies Hobbies, many parents are rediscovering hobby shops. They think hobbies are a nice alternative in this digital age of computers and electronic devices, giving kids the hands-on experience of making something they can call their own. "They actually learn something in a store like this," said Mary Brown. "We don't use that nasty word 'education' when we're talking to them, but we do emphasize that to the parents. In order for a child to build a model, he has to learn to read, he has to know a little bit of math, he has to learn patience." In fact, Brown's own children are an excellent example of the educational benefits of hobbies. All six of them shared their father's love for model airplanes, and almost all of them chose engineering as a career.

Brown admits he is a teacher at heart, always doling out help and advice to anyone who asks. Good thing, too, for it is one of the reasons people keep coming back to the store. On most days, there is a steady stream of people coming in with half-built projects, vehicles crashed to pieces, or maybe just a confused look on their face. And although Brownies offers practically any item a hobbyist could want, it is the customer service and friendliness of the Brown family that keeps customers coming back. "When somebody's finished a transaction with us and they're ready to leave, they actually shake Brownie's hand or my hand," said Mary Brown. "I always think to myself, 'Do they do that in Kmart?'"

HOLTERMANN'S BAKERY

Established in 1878

405 Arthur Kill Road, Great Kills, Staten Island
718-984-7095
Bus: S54, S74, or X15 to Arthur Kill Road–Giffords Lane
Open Sunday–Monday: 7:30 a.m. to 4:30 p.m.
Tuesday–Saturday: 7:30 a.m. to 6:00 p.m.

Anyone who has lived on Staten Island for any amount of time knows about Holtermann's Bakery. This local institution can lay just as much claim to the island as the Verrazano-Narrows Bridge or Staten Island Ferry. Opened in 1878, Holtermann's has been owned and operated all this time by the same family.

Claus Holtermann, newly emigrated from Hanover, Germany, decided to make his mark in his new country with his baking skills. Family members helped out while Holtermann went door-to-door selling loaves of bread out of his horse-and-buggy. The business gradually grew to include dozens of different kinds of baked goods and a fleet of deliverymen. For decades, Holtermann's orange-and-blue trucks and neatly uniformed drivers were a fixture on Staten Island. At one point, the shop was baking more than 5,000 loaves of bread daily. Holtermann's stopped doing home deliveries in 1978, but before that it was one of the last companies in America still doing them.

The delivery trucks are gone now—although the family keeps one in the garage for posterity—but Holtermann's still buzzes with activity. It is still a family affair, with parents and children working long hours side-by-side. Owner Clifford Holtermann, now in his 80s, still comes in almost every day. "I started here when I was about 14, and I used to work part time after school," he said. "I graduated from high school, and then I went to college for a couple of years, and my father said, 'You want to be a baker?' So I decided to come into the baking business, and I've been here for 60 years. I'm trying to retire if I can, to turn it over to my children. I just felt that my father worked so hard, I wanted to keep it going in memory of him. I know he would appreciate that."

As for the bakery, it too has aged well. Much of the interior is the same as when the shop moved to its current location in the 1930s. Many of the baking tools and machines are vintage, making the place look like a museum dedicated to the art of baking. Some of the machines are so old they have to have special parts made for them. The Holtermanns still use much of the original equipment because it works and because simple is always better.

All the shop's baked goods are made from scratch with basic, wholesome ingredients. Most of its products are so fresh and pure that they have a very limited shelf life. Some 200 different items are made at Holtermann's—from coffee cakes, rolls, strudels, and jelly doughnuts to its famous crumb buns.

Sundays are particularly packed with customers; they even line up outside before the shop opens. "It's like a special day for us," said Jill Holtermann, Clifford's daughter. "We make our specialty items—certain doughnuts, certain rolls. Onion rolls are only available on the weekends. People go to church, they come here, and they pick up their goods. There's sometimes a line before the sun even comes up."

According to the family, the shop is about more than providing the world with pastries. It is also one family's creative expression that has lasted through generations. "I want a younger generation to say they remember Holtermann's, too," said Jill. "I want people to enjoy our family, our history, and our food."

KILLMEYER'S
OLD BAVARIA INN

Established in 1888

4254 Arthur Kill Road, Charleston, Staten Island
www.killmeyers.com 718-984-1202
Bus: S74 Bus to Arthur Kill Road–Arden Avenue
Open Monday–Thursday: 11:00 a.m. to 10:00 p.m.
Friday–Saturday: 11:00 a.m. to 11:00 p.m.
Sunday: 12:00 p.m. to 9:00 p.m.

One must meander through a winding wooded road—a rarity in all of the city's boroughs—in order to get to Killmeyer's, which is located in the bucolic neighborhood of Charleston in Staten Island. Once called Kreischerville, this area used to be a thriving German immigrant neighborhood known for its breweries and brick factory. Today, little remains of its German heritage and the breweries and brick factory are gone. The name Kreischerville was changed to Charleston during World War I due to anti-German sentiment.

Luckily, Killmeyer's has survived the neighborhood's various transformations over the decades and remains a truly authentic German restaurant. The building itself is picturesque, looking every bit like a tavern. Upon entering the front door, one is immediately ensconced by the trappings of an authentic Bavarian eatery. There are dark wood walls and rich tones, making the restaurant feel like a cozy den. The main dining rooms are filled with German decorations and decor, and, of course, there is mustard on every table. The waitresses wear brightly colored *dirndls*, a traditional dress from Bavaria.

The building's history is a long one. Sections of it go back to the 1700s, when the neighborhood was still sprawling farmland. The building housed its first business in 1859, when Nicholas Killmeyer, a Bavarian immigrant, opened up a general store and barbershop. Around 1888, his sons, Albert and Theodore, took the business over and turned it into Killmeyer's Union Hotel, with rooms for rent upstairs and a bar and restaurant on the ground floor. The Killmeyer family owned the tavern until 1945. Next, the Simonson family stepped in and renamed it Rube's. In 1959, the name was changed to The Century Inn. The place gradually transformed into a popular roadhouse with a thriving music scene. During the 1970s and '80s, many popular New Jersey–area rock bands played here, including Twisted Sister.

Then, in 1995, restaurateur Ken Tirado, along with two business partners, decided to buy the place from Cap Simonson. Tirado's goal was always to turn the place back into a proper German restaurant. Starting practically from scratch, the owners gave the place a top-to-bottom renovation. Slowly but surely they brought back its 19th-century charms while throwing away remnants of previous eras, like a disco ball, generations of linoleum floor tile, and chicken wire on the windows from its roadhouse days. The renovations revealed hidden gems like the original maple flooring, an ornate tin ceiling covered by a drop ceiling, and even long-forgotten fireplaces covered up by sheet rock.

The best piece is the mahogany bar from 1890, standing dignified with its rich, dark woods and 19th-century hand-carved flourishes, including the Killmeyer's nameplate. Behind the bar are original ice block–cooled refrigerators retrofitted with an electric refrigerated system. Another original element is the tap system, which is simply a set of steel coils that are packed with ice. Beer is passed through the coils, giving what many beer aficionados insist is a cooler, more refreshing taste. The bar serves beers from Austria, Belgium, Czech Republic, and Holland, just to name a few. At any given time, there are more than a dozen beers on draft.

Over the years, Tirado and his wife, Elise, have acquired German and breweriana ephemera, giving the restaurant even more of an authentic feel. There are several one-of-a-kind items that were used at the German Pavilion at the 1964 World's Fair, including beer tap barrels, flags, and tapestries. This authenticity continues with The Happy Tones, a genuine oompah band that plays here regularly on weekends, and with the outdoor beer garden behind the restaurant.

Though the German decor is plentiful, Killmeyer's is really known more for its food. Ken Tirado went all out, hiring an authentic German chef and visiting the country several times. The menu is classic German fare: sauerbraten, rouladen, and wiener schnitzel. The restaurant's sausages are especially popular, like smoked bratwurst, weibwurst, kielbasa, and blutwurst, all of which are freshly made by a local German butcher.

Tirado tells newcomers not to be afraid of German food. "It's basic, hearty, meat-and-potatoes food. Wiener schnitzel is really just a veal cutlet; schnitzel is just a pounded breaded cutlet; jagerschnitzel is a pork cutlet with mushroom gravy on it. No one is going to give you monkey brains," he said.

Walking by the St. George Theatre on Hyatt Street in Staten Island, one could easily mistake it for just another old building. Its grey and somewhat plain exterior gives little hint of the visual delights inside. With its lobby and theater dripping with splendid decorations and trimmings, the interior of St. George is a feast for the eyes.

The theater is a classic movie and entertainment palace, built in an era when people still dressed up to go out to the movies. A time when pretty usherettes escorted patrons to their seats and a three-reeler was standard. A time when an entire community came out for the local premiere of the next blockbuster.

The St. George was built to rival the theaters of Broadway, costing what was then an exorbitant sum—half a million dollars. It was built in 1929 by architects Eugene DeRosa and James Whitford, who used a mix of Spanish and Italian baroque themes. Oversized murals, grand staircases, ornate fountains, and gilded carved figurines and decorations are stuffed in every nook and cranny. The theater also features one of the largest cantilever balconies ever built. At one time, the theater could seat some 3,000 people, who would see an assortment of entertainment that included first-run movies, musical performances, and vaudeville shows. Among the many performers were Kate Smith, Al Jolson, and Arthur Godfrey.

The theater had a good economical life until the end of the 1960s, but fell into disrepair soon after, with the last movie playing in 1972. Through the years the theater underwent several incarnations to keep it afloat, including a night club, antique showroom, and even a roller rink. Unfortunately, none of them stuck and the theater was shuttered for nearly three decades. In the mid-1990s, it reopened for a time as a performing arts center, but unfortunately economic problems soon forced its closure.

But then, in 2004, a guardian angel came into the picture and the St. George Theatre's fate was changed forever. That angel was a woman by the name of Rosemary Cappozalo, well-known in Staten Island for her patronage to the arts and a dance instructor who taught generations of local girls, some of whom went on to become Radio City Rockettes or dancers on Broadway.

"She not only taught dance; she was the most giving person you would want to meet," said Doreen Cugno, Cappozalo's daughter. "She used her life savings, more than one million dollars, to help begin the restoration of this theater. She donated it all."

Cappozalo and her three daughters quickly went to work—putting in a new roof, upgrading the electrical, plumbing, heating, and cooling systems, and painting 80 percent of the building. "We didn't realize the amount of work that really had to be done until we stepped in here," said Cugno. "We'd probably still take on the project, but we would have prepared ourselves a little better."

During the restoration, the women discovered old movie stills and posters, which they have now proudly put back up. And with the theater back to its original grandeur, the St. George is serving Staten Island even better as both a performing arts and community center, with more than 100 performances and 100,000 people visiting yearly. Some of the recent performers at the theater include Howie Mandel, Tracy Morgan, and Tony Bennett. The St. George has also been used in film shoots, including the television show *Gossip Girl* and the movie *School of Rock*.

Unfortunately, just a few months shy of the grand reopening of the theater, Cappozalo—who had been battling cancer—passed away. Now, her daughters are intent on fulfilling her biggest wish and keeping her legacy alive. "We have made it a priority that this theater is for everyone. We have outreach programs for children, teens, adults, and seniors so everyone can have the opportunity to see a show," said Cugno. The daughters are also continuing their mother's work by giving free dance lessons to underprivileged kids. And through Cappozalo's generosity of restoring the St. George Theatre, countless others will be touched by her for years to come.

ST. GEORGE THEATRE

Established in 1929

35 Hyatt Street
St. George, Staten Island
www.stgeorgetheatre.com
Box office: 718-442-2900
Located near Staten Island
Ferry Terminal
Open Monday–Friday:
9:30 a.m. to 2:00 p.m.
Closed weekends
unless show is scheduled.

ACKNOWLEDGMENTS

FIRST AND FOREMOST, I WOULD LIKE TO THANK
ALL OF THE OWNERS AND EMPLOYEES OF THE BUSINESSES
I PROFILED FOR *NEW YORK ORIGINALS* FOR THEIR
APPRECIATION AND ENTHUSIASM FOR THIS PROJECT.

AT RIZZOLI, A BIG THANK-YOU TO JIM MUSCHETT
FOR TAKING ON THE PROJECT, AND MY EDITOR,
CANDICE FEHRMAN, WHO WAS WONDERFUL AT FINE-TUNING
MY TEXT AND KEEPING THE WHOLE PROCESS
ORDERLY AND STRESS-FREE. (AT LEAST FOR ME!)

NEXT, THANK YOU TO WILLY WONG, THE BOOK DESIGNER,
WHO—AS YOU WILL SEE—CREATED THE
PERFECT BALANCE OF NOSTALGIA AND STYLE TO MAKE
THE BOOK A RELEVANT AND INTERESTING READ.

THANK YOU ALSO TO THE EMPLOYEES AT
THE APPLE STORE FIFTH AVENUE
AND B & H PHOTO AND VIDEO,
WHO WERE ALWAYS MORE THAN HAPPY
TO ANSWER MY TECHNICAL QUESTIONS.

AND LAST, THANK YOU
TO ALL THE
PBS STATIONS
WHO HAVE CARRIED MY
NEW YORK ORIGINALS
TELEVISION SERIES
ON THEIR CHANNELS.
SEE YOU NEXT SEASON!